A Memoir of
Hayawo Kiyama

My
Way

我が道

My
Way

A Memoir of
Hayawo Kiyama

Christine Willis

Irene Weinberger Books
An imprint of Hamilton Stone Editions
Maplewood, New Jersey

My Way: A Memoir of Hayawo Kiyama
© 2025 Christine Willis

ISBN: 978-1-7365001-9-4

Back Cover Photograph, Kumamoto Castle: Goro Kato

Irene Weinberger Books
An Imprint of Hamilton Stone Editions
Maplewood, New Jersey
P.O. Box 43, Maplewood, NJ 07040
ireneweinbergerbooks.com   hamiltonstone.org

Appreciation to Goro Kato for the many hours of interpreting.

早飯
早糞
早走り

Eat Fast,
Shit Fast,
Run Fast.

Contents

Introduction xiii

I. Kumamoto 1
  Kiyama Family Lifestyle 1
    Learning to Share 1
    Okasan 2
    Otosan 6
    Home Life 11
    Bath 14
    Food 14
    Health 16
    Teeth 16
  War: The Reality 18
    Hunger Deepens 18
    School and the Lessons of War 20
    Warnings, Bites, and Burns 24
    Nagasaki: An Unutterable Ending August 9, 1945 25
    End of War, August 15, 1945 27
  After the War 30
    Unscathed by War but Changed by Barbers 30

On Japanese Soil: American Soldiers 31
I, Hunting Dog 33
Night Soil—An Accident 35
Judo "*Shut Up*" 36
    Training 38
    Judo Gi 40
    The Black Belt 42
    A Dangling Eyeball 45
Yakuza: 1956 46
Animals 47
School After the War 50
    Discipline 50
    Competition 52
    Rabbit Hunting 53
    Dairy Work 54
Working in the Family Rice Processing Business 55
    Delivery Boy 55
    My Father's Mistake, My Future 56
    My Business Responsibility 57
    My Work 58

Chapter II: Making a Life Decision 63
Tradition: Atotsugi and Generosity 63
Leaving Kumamoto 66

Chapter III: 1960–1963 August to August
Delano, California 69
    Arrival 69
    Life in Delano 70
    Vineyard Prostitution 72
    Resignation 73
Lessons on the Central Coast of California 73
    Startled! 73
    Mr. and Mrs. Eto: First Generation 76
    Domestic Life in Camp 78
    Laboring on the Farm 80
        Learning the Ropes 80
        Camp 82
        Pressure 84

    The Work Environment..85
        Mr. Eto, the Man...87
        Driver's License 87
        While I Worked: The News, Local and World 88
        Illegal and Illegals...89
        Cheating Mexicans 91
        Accident and Rehab..92
        Communication 93

Chapter IV: First Work Tour Concludes....................................... 95
    Planning to Return 95

Chapter V: Return to Japan... 101
    Disappointment 101
        1963–1965 101
    Homecoming! Banzai!... 103
    Mitsui Miiki Coal Mine Disaster 106
    Finding a Profession and Finding a Wife.............................. 107
        Spring Light Garden 107
        Struggle to Get the Girl 109
        Getting Married.. 111
        Lessons of Grandparents and Susumu......................... 112
        Transitioning 116
        Los Angeles before the Next Reality 117

Chapter VI: Returning to the Farm with a Pregnant Wife.... 121
    A Farm Worker's Family Life 1966–1970 121
    Husband, Wife, Children, and Earning a Living.................... 121
    Taxes 126
    Disasters.. 127
    Tempted: The Doctor.. 129
    Becoming Independent 131

Chapter VII: Independence... 133
    The Buddhist Temple House 133
    Temple House to Los Osos House 138
    Judo on the Central Coast 141

Chapter VIII: Life as a Gardener 149
    Gardening 149

Faith's Position; My Position 152
Railroad Ties 155
Spyglass and Sunset 157

Chapter IX: Aiki-Jujitsu 159
The Japanese Aiki World 159
Aiki-jujutsu in the United States 162

Chapter X: Becoming Old, But Still Becoming 167
Approaching Sixty-nine Years Old,
and the Driving Test: Again! 167
Guests, Giri, and Gratitude 169
    Visitors and Giri 169
    Gratitude 171
My Seventieth Birthday: August 26, 2006 172

Chapter XI: Concluding Thoughts 175

Introduction

My family and I met Mr. Hayawo Kiyama, (Ken, to most Americans), at the Wisteria Festival held at the Buddhist Temple in San Luis Obispo, CA, in 1993. Mr. Kiyama and his Coastal Judo Club members were performing a demonstration of various techniques practiced at their club in part to maintain and increase membership. We three were in the audience: Goro, my husband; Alex, our son who was eight years old at the time; and I. Goro and I thought that Alex might become interested in judo. And indeed, after watching the judoists perform, that day he determined to take judo lessons. Over a very short period, a family friendship began to develop with Mr. Kiyama.

Mr. Kiyama's journey to the United States was a circuitous one. He was born in Kumamoto, Japan, August 26, 1936, but as a young man with familial financial obligations, he immigrated to the United States to take advantage of the strong dollar. After many years of struggle, both in Japan and the United States, he ultimately became a citizen of the United States and began his own judo and aiki-jujitsu dojo.

Mr. Kiyama's dojo was in a rather remote area of the Central Coast of California. The first time we decided to visit the club, Mr. Kiyama's wife, Faith, gave us verbal directions over the phone assuring us, with all the assurance of one who has mastered a route, that we could not miss it. From San Luis Obispo, take Route 1, turn right across from Cuesta College, follow the road (its narrowness and winding nature amid fields of brown did not instill confidence in our ability to find the dojo) until you come to a gate (there was more than one gate), turn right, go across a bridge (just a tad larger than foot bridge width), and continue to follow the road until you see an old army building. We gave up when we came to the second gate, which was locked. Another day, however, with perseverance, we found our way and learned that the gate had to be unlocked by a member with a key. But it was well worth the second effort to locate the dojo. The surrounding dojo area was alive with wild turkeys, an occasional bobcat, random wild boar, deer, and most endearing, hundreds of starlings who had made nests all around and under the dojo roof. (Not so endearing was evidence of their existence directly below their nests.)

The dojo building was on loan from the military: an old clapboard building with uncertain plumbing and electricity. It was not necessary to heat the building as even on the coldest evenings in this mild climate, the judoists soon became comfortable through the exertion of practice. Wooden steps led up into a waiting room separated from the practice area by a door and a wooden wall with the upper half glass for viewing the practice. Immediately upon entry, a distinctive odor of rotting wood, bare feet, sweat, and tatami mats was evident. (In earlier years, there were no traditional tatami mats but rather one large mat filled with sawdust and newspaper.) A table had been positioned in the middle of the waiting room for parents and younger siblings of the children's class's students. The county, who loaned the land and building, required that a children's class be taught for Mr. Kiyama to have possession of the building rent-free.

Goro would go into the practice area and with great interest watch the warm-ups and matches. Soon after Alex started lessons, Mr. Kiyama, eager to speak in Japanese, would abandon teaching to his assistant, Dwayne, and spend time talking with Goro. This conversation was always conducted on the sidelines and in Japanese, Mr. Kiyama's and Goro's native tongue. I remained in the waiting room with a few other parents.

For many months we had traveled to the dojo on Monday and Wednesday evenings for the children's class from 6:00 to 7:00 p.m. A few years later, Alex joined the adult class, which ran from 7:00 until 9:00 p.m. Mr. Kiyama and Goro began to realize that they had much

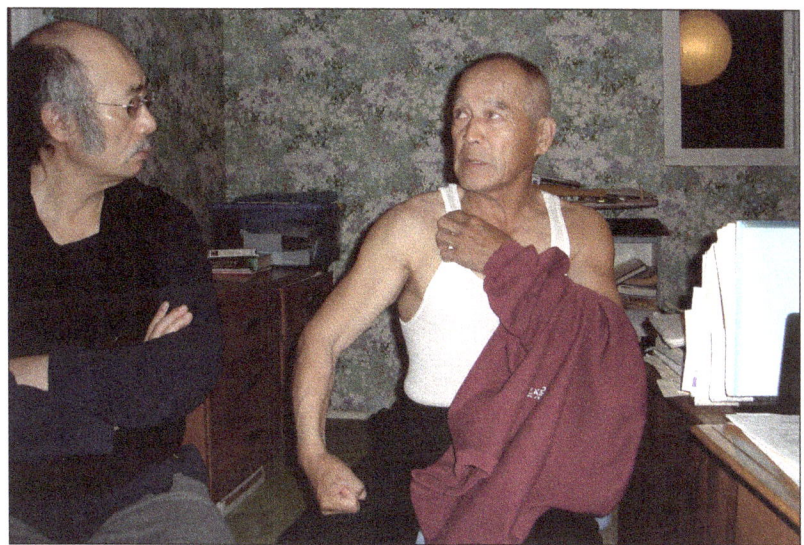

Mr. Kiyama telling his stories.

more to talk about than could be accomplished during the judo class, so Mr. Kiyama began driving from the dojo after the adult class to our house for more conversation. The conversations were animated and prolonged, often lasting until 2:00 a.m.

We three marveled at the richness and vitality of Mr. Kiyama's life: our lives, by comparison, appeared cautious and safe. It would be unconscionable to allow his stories to go untold, so, determined to take advantage of his frequent visits, each Thursday night, on which there were no judo or aiki classes held, Mr. Kiyama would come at 6:30 p.m., and he, Goro, and I would climb the stairs in our house to my office on the second floor where Mr. Kiyama would relate, in Japanese, his life's stories. Little prompting was required to launch Mr. Kiyama into verbally reliving his life story: I would remind him where we had left off the previous week, and with alert and animated expression, he would continue reliving his life experiences. Goro would interpret, and I would type. After the note taking sessions, Goro and Mr. Kiyama would go to the dining room table, and Goro would serve Mr. Kiyama a small meal of brown rice, a vegetable miso stew, and green tea. As the evening progressed, they would move into the family room to watch sumo wrestling on NHK or a drama in Japanese. The relationship continued to evolve over time.

—Christine Willis

One

Kumamoto

Kiyama Family Lifestyle

LEARNING TO SHARE

"Are you ready to share?!" My father shouted. Taisei, one of my younger brothers not yet in first grade, had been fighting over food with my youngest sister, Chieko. Chieko wanted half of what Taisei was eating, but he refused saying he would eat it all. My father grabbed both of Taisei's legs, turned him upside down, and carried him that way to the back yard koi pond. My father dunked my brother's head into the pond, holding him there until he was gasping for breath, pulled him out, and demanded, "Are you ready to share?!" My brother said he was not, and my father dunked him again. With the third dunking, my brother gave up and through tears said that he would share. He cried because he had been put in the dirty water and had drunk lots of it. After my father had shouted at Taisei three times, "Boys don't cry!" and Taisei continued crying, he told him that if he didn't quit, he would be hit and dunked into the water again. My mother, as wife and mother, could only stand by and watch: not until my father had left, could she offer comfort.

OKASAN

My mother, Tanae, delivered all seven of her children at home often while my father was away at work. My sisters were allowed to be present during the birth, but the boys were not allowed anywhere near the birthing room. When my mother was about to give birth to my younger siblings, my job was to go get the midwife and give her a ride to my house on the back of my bicycle. If the birth were difficult or long, she would stay overnight or sometimes two nights.

When I heard the newborn baby's first cry, I was responsible for preparing warm water in a large tub. After the water was ready, I got the *surikogi* 擂粉木 (pestle), so that my grandmother could prepare a traditional breast poultice that encouraged the milk to come out. She took dried carp scales and skin and put them into the *suribachi* 擂鉢 (mortar) with the surikoge, and my job was to steadily hold the bowl while my grandmother ground the carp scales. After grinding them into a powder, she blended in wheat flour and water to make a paste. She then put the paste on rice paper with a hole for my mother's nipple; after applying the paste and paper to the breasts, my grandmother would place a warm moist towel on top of the poultice and around each breast and massage them. She would then wrap the breasts in a soft material for two days: the breasts became softer, and milk started to come out.

My brothers and I were curious to see the new baby, but my grandmother would say, "Not yet, not yet." Eventually, when my mother was ready, we would be allowed in to see the new baby. It was a good tradition to let the mother decide when the other children could come and see the baby. I wanted to touch the baby's cheeks, but my grandmother would only allow me to after I'd washed my hands, and soon after I had to give the midwife a ride home. I was very involved with the birth of my siblings.

No cow milk or formula was available for feeding a baby, so there was no option but for my mother to nurse. My mother nursed me for two years. About every two years another child was born, so she began nursing the younger child. She nursed each of her children about two years, so in all, she nursed nearly fourteen years. Her breasts were always out, and she was always producing milk. She tried to eat well by eating *niboshi* 煮干し (small, dried fish) so that her milk would be nutritious. She put miso in a pan with hot water and together with the fish poured the mixture over white rice: the small fish provided her with calcium because she ate the bones. Except for the times there was a teacher visiting or a formal guest we had not previously met, my mother would nurse in front of her friends, family, neighbor girls, boys, and even adult men. There was no embarrassment. At this time, no women wore bras. They wore a very thin chemise with a loose cup-like area, and it made nursing easy. My mother just opened her kimono and nursed. She would talk with her visitors and serve tea as she fed her children: since she was wearing a kimono, which had no fasteners, she didn't need to unbutton any clothing. It was very easy to nurse, and no one was uncomfortable because she was nursing. She continued talking when she was feeding, stopping to change from one breast to the other and then talk again. My mother did not worry over small details. It was completely natural for her to nurse on the train or anywhere else.

My mother would spray milk on the baby's face before she began to nurse as a sign to "Be ready." And if an older child complained of having something in an eye that caused irritation, she would hold the eye open, aim her breast, and squirt milk straight into the eye. My father thought this was a bad idea, but she said that breast milk was good for everything. If one of us had pink eye, she would squirt milk into the eye and rub it in. She told us that would clean the eye.

When I was ten years old and food was scarce, my siblings and I would sit in *seiza* 正座 (kneeling: the tops of the feet are on the floor) position. We would wait with our mouths open, and my mother would squeeze breast milk into each of our mouths. Sometimes she would miss, and as we watched each other, we would wipe our faces with our hands and lick the milk off. Thanks to this experience when I was ten, I can recall the sweet taste of human milk. When she was finished, she would pat each of us and say *futonara* (ふとなら) twice, a Kyushu term meaning *to grow up big*. When her milk began to dwindle, she fed only the babies.

Sharing milk with all the children was rather unique to my mother. But she was unusually maternal, and her kindness extended beyond her own family. A neighbor had a mentally handicapped baby, Tsuneo Kikumoto, and he was very skinny. His mother didn't have any milk, so he was crying from hunger all the time. My mother nursed Tsuneo first but saved enough milk to feed my younger brother who was still nursing. For one year, every day she fed Tsuneo at 3:00 p.m. Since her own baby had to share her breast milk, she supplemented his nutrition with a soup-like rice mixture.

My mother worked all the time and rarely sat down. With so many children, she had to cook and clean all day, every day. But even with all her duties, she still found time to treat us in a special way, even for a small achievement, by making it clear that a particular food had been made for a certain child's achievement. She would also take time to listen to all our secrets, but if my father came in during the sharing of a secret, she made everyone get quiet.

As a child, I got the feeling that my mother enjoyed watching her children grow. She was very affectionate to all of us. She would ask me how my Japanese language was coming along at school. I would tell her that it was not going along very well, but that I was doing very well in PE. I had one subject that I was doing very well in, and she supported me in that without criticizing any failure, so I felt good about myself.

I was aware that when my mother went to the bathroom in the middle of the night, she always checked on us children. If a cover were off, she would replace it. I was often awakened when she came in. She talked to us children when we were sleeping, softly whispering: "Be a good boy," "Grow up healthy," "Good girl." She was almost talking to herself; even now it moves me to remember. My mother had a tremendous love for her children. When I think of her, I think first of her loving attitude toward her children. My mother did not give the impression that she was strong, but she was gentle, soft, open-minded, and tender. She was my teacher: I realize that now because the way I parent is similar to the way she parented. When I go back home, my old friends tell me my face is more and more like my mother's, and that my face is the closest to my mother's face of all my brothers and sisters.

My mother understood that her role as a wife was to be obedient to her husband. She always agreed with my father in front of him, but sometimes out of his presence she would shake her fist in frustration. If he reappeared, she became quiet again. My father didn't physically abuse her, but he shouted at her frequently. Sometimes he would shout when my mother had not completed errands he had asked her to run, but my mother had seven children, and sometimes she wouldn't be able to run errands, or she would forget. Then he got upset. He didn't shout often, but we children had an expression, "Last night the thunder was big," meaning my father had been shouting. When my father would yell nasty things at my mother, she would tell us children to go to our rooms for a while. She would then excuse herself, walk away, and wait until his anger subsided. He would read the newspaper and begin to calm down, and once he stopped being angry, he'd feel embarrassed at how he had acted. She knew the right timing to serve him green tea after such an event. Sometimes I speak harshly to my wife, just as my father did to my mother. I fear I may end up apologizing to her on my deathbed. I hit my wife once in 1993, but she started to call the cops, and that was the last time I hit her. Times have changed: now she tells me to shut up when she doesn't like something I've said, but I still feel sorry for having hit her.

My mother, Tanae.

My mother considered my father a good husband because even though he had many meetings to attend, he always came home for dinner. As he was leaving for business meetings, my mother would check for lint on his shoulder. She would adjust his sleeves, neatly bend his collar, and straighten his necktie. She polished his shoes and put a shoehorn next to them ready for him to use. Once he put his shoes on, she would see him off at the gate and ask him what time he expected to be back. Then she would say, "Now go."

Although my parents did not use affectionate words to each other nor was there any kissing or hugging between them in front of others, they were strongly connected and understood each other. The only demonstrative affection between them was the daily massage my mother would give my father. (My brother, Dairoku, helped by walking on my father's back as part of the massage.) My family members communicated well, and we all felt very close.

OTOSAN

There was a twelve-year age gap between my mother and father. My father, Tetsuro (whose name means Iron Man), first married my mother's sister, Sunae, with whom he had three children. When she died, her children were still young and needed a mother, and my father married her sister, Tanae, my mother.

My father's family members were mostly merchants, and during my father's youth, most people didn't get an education beyond the eighth grade. My grandfather decided that my father should stop school after fourth grade to become a merchant, but my father had wanted to finish the sixth grade. One day, with a great deal of pride, he showed me the correspondence courses he had taken to complete the sixth grade. My grandfather did give an educational opportunity to his oldest son, however, and my father, the second son, believed that his father felt his brother was brighter. My grandfather treated my father differently from his brother, and my father didn't take it well; in fact, he didn't like it at all.

When my father was twenty years old, he asked his father for 5,000 yen to buy a *seimai* 精米 (grain refinement machine) for a business he planned to start. My grandfather lent him the money, but he insisted that my father write him an IOU; he told my father that the money was not a gift, and that he must return it.

My father went to his father's house every month to pay him, and it took ten years to return the 5,000 yen. When my father was ready to pay the last month's installment, he was determined to end his relationship with his parents. He planned to throw the money down in anger in front of his father and ask him how much interest he owed. His older brother had gotten lots of money from their parents for his education without an IOU, and my father felt his parents were treating him like a stranger. He was extremely angry at the difference in treatment. He went to his parents' house, and just before he began to express his anger, they took him to the small Buddhist shrine in their house to offer a prayer.

After the prayer, they guided him to the dining area where he found a special meal had been prepared for him. There was tai fish and a full dinner ready. My father defiantly said, "I'm not hungry." My grandfather poured sake; my father didn't want to accept the drink, but he planned never to see them after this night, so he thought he might as well drink. As he drank the sake, his father brought out a thin notebook and handed it to my father. He told him that it was a receipt book in which he had kept a record of repayment, and he told him to look at it. My father said that he would look at it when he got it to his own home. Then his father brought out a savings account booklet and explained that each time my father had paid him, the next day, he would take the money to the post office bank and put the payment in an account in my father's name. The 5,000 yen was returned to my father plus interest. My grandfather said that my father had proved that he was a capable man, and both of his parents clapped their hands. They said that his hard work and dedication guaranteed he would be able to live independently, and they all cried. This is the old-fashioned way of educating a child.

Refinement building and employees. My mother is seated in the first row on the ground holding my younger sister, Hiroko. My father is behind my mother, and his mother is beside him on his right. I am the baby being held in the middle row to the left of the Japanese flag.

Dairoku (my brother) and the family business. This picture shows the size of our business which included all buildings visible on Dairoku's left.

My father did end up having a big success in the refinement business; in fact, at one time, we owned six houses including the one we lived in. My father provided a milling service for our prefecture and exported milled rice to other prefectures. Five or six trucks full of rice arrived at our house every day during the harvest season. He bought one house after another that he converted into grain warehouses because so much rice was being delivered to him for refining. We also had nine machines. This is how my father ended up focused on the business world.

I think that the way my father was raised determined the type of man and father he would be.

When I was a child, my father was immersed in Japanese society. A cultural expectation was to not express his emotions publicly, especially anger. However, he could and would let his anger out on his family. And when it came to my performance in school, there were many occasions for anger. Teachers visited their students' homes at that time, and my teachers would often tell my parents during those visits that I had not learned my lessons and did not do my homework.

After the teacher left, my father would shout his disappointment and anger yelling, "Don't shame me!"

My father felt he had been cheated out of an education as a child, so education became a major focus of his parenting. He must have been worried about my academic abilities, because when I was six years old, he took me to the Dazaifu-Tenmangu Shrine, a Shinto shrine dedicated to the divine scholar, Michizane Sugawara. It was believed that if a parent took a child to this shrine, the child would have a better brain. I don't recall what my fortune was on the *omikuji* 御神籤 (a piece of paper that one drew from a box at a shrine or at a temple that predicted the person's future), but I remember my father prayed for me to become a star general; generals were paid a huge salary, and my father wanted me to become a high ranked officer and serve my country.

But he didn't wait passively for his prayers to be answered. My father would line all seven of us children up in front of him and quiz us on arithmetic problems. I was always the last to raise my hand because I became nervous and froze when quizzed, but my sisters

Noodle making. Soumen noodle making was also part of my father's business, and this is the area the noodles were made.

were quick. Hiroko, two years younger than I, was the quickest: she knew the answer before our father finished the question. My father said that it would have been better if she had been born the oldest male, and that I had been born the youngest child. All three girls took after my father: they had strong bodies and quick brains.

In my family, each of the boys took a bath with our father, and it was there where the arithmetic quizzes continued. When it was my turn, if I missed a problem, he would shout, "Study harder" and then slap me in the face. My father would follow up by reminding me that my school failures had embarrassed him at PTA meetings. I would often have to apologize to him in the bath. My younger brother, Futoru, was good at language and arithmetic, and my oldest and youngest sisters were both good in these subjects. My father knew that I was good at PE and sports, so he would ask me how I did in those activities. He was generous with his praise regarding these successes, so I was eager to tell him of my sporting successes. But my father was severe when it came to academic subjects.

After many arithmetic sessions lined up with my siblings and in the bath, one PTA school visiting-day, my father attended Mr. Nakajima's arithmetic class, my teacher's class. Many parents were observing on that day as well as my father. Mr. Nakajima wrote a problem on the board and asked who could solve it. I was eager to impress my father, so I shot my hand up fast. I should have figured the problem out first, but I didn't and couldn't answer. Mr. Nakajima recognized that I was trying to show off for my father, and he became angry and said aloud that I should be embarrassed. When we got home, my father hit me in the head with his fist. Along with the pain of being hit, I got a loud and long lecture. My father didn't control his strength when he hit me, and he would call me names. Once the pain was gone and the lecture over, I didn't dwell on the fact that my father had hit me. A bump appeared on my head after I was hit, and I could tell that he was worried because he told my mother to put a cold towel on it. After my father left the house, my mother explained why my father hit me. She assured me that my father liked me, and that I shouldn't be upset; I felt free to cry in front of my mother after my father was gone. Of all my brothers, I was hit the most.

My father's education of us children went beyond arithmetic and included lessons to ensure we spoke with confidence. At home, if we

My father, Tetsuro, 1950.

didn't respond clearly enough or with conviction to a question my father asked, he would get angry and make us repeat the response loudly until he was satisfied. We could not give wishy-washy answers. This parental treatment was similar in all families of our social class at this time in Kyushu, even though my father may have been a bit extreme.

My father impacted my life greatly, but his most significant impact on me came later in my life and determined the direction my life would take.

HOME LIFE

Our two-story house was old-fashioned and very traditional with a wooden hallway and *shoji* 障子 (paper screen used on wooden frame) door. We had seven rooms including a dining room and kitchen, and *tatami* 畳 mats (soft woven reed mats used in traditional homes) that covered wood floors. The frame of the house was made of wood; clay mixed with straw provided insulation. The outside was wood, so the insulating clay and straw weren't visible. Because it is very humid in Kumamoto, we had a crawl space measuring about two feet deep under the floor that allowed air to circulate making the house more comfortable in summer.

We didn't have a refrigerator, so we used an area beneath the house for produce preservation. We dug a hole six feet deep and eight feet wide under the foyer. A wooden door in the floor led to steps under the floor. We stored sweet potatoes, daikon (radish), and Irish potatoes, and they could last six to ten months. When there was leftover cooked rice, we put it in a bamboo container and placed it in a high place in the basement on the north side where the air circulated, and it could last a day. This method substituted for refrigeration. There were no iceboxes for residential houses, but some stores sold ice that had been made in a factory. The ice factory workers didn't cut through the block of ice but would cut a line, and then the fish sellers used an ice pick to make small pieces to keep their fish fresh.

Refrigeration was not much of a problem in the cold winter, but over a twenty-year period, I only recall one snow in Kumamoto. We lived near the beach, and the wind would blow snow over the mountain. But the days in winter were cold, clear but cold. And the nights were even colder. We had no centralized heating in our house, so we each wore a cotton *hanten* 半纏 (a short, padded jacket worn inside the house) during the winter. In the family room, we had a *kotatsu* 炬燵 (a table with a heating element underneath) that burned *rentan* 練炭 (charcoal), but that was the only heat source in our house. When we children slept, we each had extra covers, and we kept our feet warm under the blanket near the *kotatsu*. But our faces were so cold, and we could see our breath. It was below freezing outside, and the fishpond in the back yard would often have one or two inches of ice. On the coldest nights, we fought over the top shared *futons* 布団 (filled mattresses used to sleep on the floor). We siblings were lined up on our futons one after the other: Futoru, Dairoku, Taisei, Saeko, Hiroko, Chieko, and I. (My aunt's three children did not sleep with us: one was in the army, the oldest sister was married, and the third slept alone.) While sleeping, we moved so much that legs and heads were all over the place, and sometimes our legs would be exposed. When were all in bed, we would kick each other under the *kotatsu* 炬燵 (foot warmer under the table) and end up squabbling. My feet would be icy cold, and I would put them on my sisters: they would get *so* mad. We slept near the only *kotatsu* in the house; my parents slept without any heat source in their room. We had enough rooms for us to sleep spread out, but because of the cold in winter, we children slept in one room. When summer finally came, the heavy winter futons were packed away, but we still all slept together under one mosquito net with the lighter summer futons spread apart. If it became too hot or too crowded, the youngest would go to our parents' room.

We had three chests of drawers placed beside each other with name tags on each drawer for our clothing. The older children got three drawers, and the younger ones got two. There was lots of space for my clothes because I only had three pairs of underpants and three undershirts. My mother was always busy washing because we had so few clothes: later, when I worked in our grain refinement business, I changed under clothes every day. Since I was the oldest of my mother's children, I got new clothes, but the younger brothers got my *o-sagari* おさがり (hand-me-downs). School uniforms, as well as other clothing, were handed down from relatives to other relatives and from one neighboring family to another.

Before bed, I would first go to the small Buddhist and Shinto shrines in my house, ring a bell saying thank you for the day, and then I would say goodnight to my parents. The children went to bed first, and if visitors were invited, they always arrived after the children had gone to bed. Sometimes my father would lie down with us using that time as an opportunity to give a lecture on morals. Usually, he just kept talking and talking, but when all the children were snoring, my father stopped talking. It was the same story over and over, and no one wanted to hear.

But the mood at bedtime on December 31 (New Year's Eve, a most important holiday for Japanese) was different: all of us children were excited when we went to bed, because we knew when we awakened on January 1, we would find a new shirt, new trousers, a new pair of *geta* 下駄 (traditional Japanese wooden sandals), and money: our *Otoshidama* お年玉 (New Year's money gifts). The age of the children determined how much they received. When I was very young, I believed that the *kamis* 神, which are similar to characters in fairy tales, delivered the gifts. All the neighbor children got *Otoshidama* gifts, but some wealthier parents could leave a heavy overcoat for their children. My mother said that we couldn't do that because we had seven children. I once asked my best friend, Takashira, if I could borrow his new coat that he had gotten as an Otoshidama gift for half a day. He let me borrow it, and it was so warm, but before I went home, I had to give it back.

BATH

It was my responsibility to pump water into the tub; filling the tub required one hundred-fifty pumps. Early in my life we used wood to heat the tub bath water, but later we switched to coal. The pump was in the kitchen where we had split bamboo poles, similar to gutters in shape that ran from the kitchen into the bath to carry the pumped water. The direction of the water could be rerouted by changing the location of the bamboo gutters. My oldest sister was responsible for heating the bath water, and if she fell behind in her duty, I would get mad at her. If she couldn't heat the water for some reason, a younger sister was responsible. If I couldn't do my job pumping water, a younger brother had to do it. Later, when I began delivering rice for my father, the younger children took over pumping water for the bath.

Everyone took a bath in the same water after having first washed outside the tub. Males bathed first, starting with the oldest one, and my mother would be the very last person to bathe. In my family, it was believed that if you let women bathe first, then the men would not amount to anything in the future, and they would never be promoted. This traditional thinking was true throughout Japan: a man should bathe ahead of a woman.

FOOD

Before the Americans joined World War II, Japan was fighting the Koreans and Chinese, but our meals were not much impacted by the military needs except that there was little rice as most of it was sent to the soldiers. And what white rice that could be bought, was very expensive. At this time, breakfast was miso soup that included a mixture of *miso* みそ (fermented soy or rice bean paste), *satsumaimo* さつまいも (sweet potato), oats, *daikon* 大根 (large white radish), and green vegetables.

Since we had no cooking gas, my mother would make miso soup on a wood fire that produced lots of smoke. Cooking done in our kitchen left soot about one inch thick that we would chisel off and take to school, add water, and make calligraphy ink out of it. My mother got up at 5:00 a.m. every morning so that she could make *bento* 弁当 (packed lunch in a box) for all of her children. The bento often included *umeboshi* 梅干し (pickled plums), *daikon*, and a combination of oats and white rice. This bento looked like a Japanese national flag because my mother put a red *umeboshi* in the center surrounded by oats and rice in a square white bento container.

Most of the fights we children had at home revolved around food, in particular, the amount of food: "I-got-less-than-you" fights. The food that most often led to squabbling was food brought home after ceremonies my parents had attended. We looked forward to the times my mother would go to a ceremony because the food she brought back was always better than we had at home. If my mother went to a wedding party and returned with a *furoshiki* 風呂敷 (a traditional wrapping cloth for carrying items) filled with food gifts, she would call all of us children and divide the treats. When there was only one portion of a food, my mother would divide it into seven pieces for the children, but the smaller the child, the more he or she got. By the time I was in junior high, my older sister and I got the least which resulted in bickering and complaining. I would protest that the little ones don't eat as much as the bigger children, and my mother would respond that the little ones had lots of catching up to do to be as big as I was.

When friends would visit, my mother bought *manju* 饅頭 (a small bun with a sweet inside) to serve. If there were not enough left over for all the children, someone had to sacrifice, and since I was the oldest of my father's second wife's children, I always had to sacrifice. It was assumed, and I accepted, that I would share with my sisters, but sometimes I would grab all the food and resist sharing with my brothers. I was the biggest and oldest boy, so my resistance was taken seriously. I would have shouting matches with my brothers, but we never hit each other. Dairoku and Futoru would grab from me what food they could, and together they would challenge me. We children annoyed each other and that was the way we communicated. Because I was the oldest son, the younger ones didn't seriously bother me. We were afraid of our father, so we didn't fight except when food was involved and then only when he was not around.

HEALTH

Even though I was afraid of my father, when I would get cut or scraped, he was the one who would treat my wounds. In my family, it was my father's job to take care of children's wounds: my father was the doctor, and my mother was the nurse. If we had a wound, he would take a chunk of salt and rub it into the wound and then wash the blood away. Then he would put salt in his palm and pat it on the wound: it was extremely painful. Tiny bubbles would appear in the entire area where the skin had been lost; he said the germs would not survive the salt, but it felt like a fire burning on the wound. As the pain grew, my father said to be patient a little longer, a little longer. The motto at that time was that boys don't cry, and my father believed in it, so if I cried when my father treated a cut or scrape with salt, I would be hit. I could run in place from pain, but I couldn't cry because boys must not cry.

Where there was construction going on, some of us children stepped on nails that would almost go through our foot: my father just pulled the nail out and took a hammer and hit the hole over and over where the nail had been in the foot. Lots of blood would flow. There were no tetanus shots available before or during the war. All children understood that the blood had to be gotten out, and I never heard of anyone who developed tetanus. Later, when I worked on a farm in the United States, wooden lettuce boxes were held together with nails that often fell out. If I stepped on a nail, the owner of the farm would give me three penicillin pills to be taken over a three-day period, but I would also force the wound to bleed. The next day it was swollen, but it was not painful.

My mother had a treatment for a pulled a muscle: she scraped ash from the bottom of a cooking pot, added water and wheat flour, and made a black poultice. She applied the black poultice and covered it with a paper cover, and it would draw the blood from deep inside the leg to just under the skin. The muscle would heal nicely.

TEETH

My father told us children that the mouth was the entrance to the body, and if you use salt to clean your teeth and gums, no cavities would develop. It was difficult to get something sweet until after the war, so in general, children's teeth were in fairly good shape anyway, but they were crooked. I had a dirty toothbrush and used a sewing thread to floss my teeth, but I cut my gums with the thread. My father believed that chewing hard foods would make your gums tough and was good for the brain.

When I was young and losing my baby teeth, my father told me to take my tongue and move the tooth left and right. After I had done this all day, he took a strong thread used for tatami mats and tied the tooth with that thread. Then, all of a sudden, he would yank, and the tooth was out. After the tooth was out, my father took lots of salt and put it in the bleeding hole. He said that if you rinse, there would be too much blood. He then made a ball from newspaper and packed the salt in the hole. He said after ten minutes take the packing out, rinse the mouth with water, and if there is still some blood, pack it one more time. After the salt and newspaper treatment, there was no more blood. This salt treatment was not painful at all. When a tooth was removed or fell out naturally, I wrapped it in newspaper, put it into a bag that my mother had made, and carried it to school to show the other children.

During the years that I was in school, a dentist came and checked our teeth twice; it took a few days for the dentist to check all the children's teeth. The school dentist did not repair our teeth, but if needed, he would give recommendations to go to a dentist to get work done. At that time, I only brushed my teeth in the morning.

Until fifteen years old, I had perfect teeth. Only black sugar, *kurozato* 黒砂糖 made from "Imo-to" (sugar from a potato), was available during the war, and I ate it straight. Many years ago, it came from Taiwan; later, I was told, it came from Hawaii. Kurozato is made from sweet potatoes that were boiled and stirred until they melted down into a sticky liquid. The liquid was then poured into a wooden barrel. As the sticky liquid lost moisture, it became very hard, and a chisel or iron stick was needed to break it. The barrel was at the store where you would break off what you wanted and weigh it. My mother used it to cook with because it was less expensive than cane sugar. It was tasty, but the sweet taste was a different sweetness from white or brown sugar. I would have a sweet potato in one hand and in the other hand sweet potato sugar. Before World War II, when I was very small, we had white, brown, and kurozato sugars available. But during and immediately after the war, there was only kurozato.

After I left school, the next time I visited the dentist I was twenty-three years old, right before I left for the United States. This time, a dentist worked on my teeth. I knew that I would not be able to afford dental care in the United States as I had been told that dentists cost a great deal more in the United States than in Japan, so I tried to get everything done before leaving home. Nothing was too seriously wrong, but the dentist numbed my mouth, cleaned out a small cavity, and filled it. My teeth were in good condition when I later left for the United States.

War: The Reality

HUNGER DEEPENS

One of my earliest and most powerful memories is of the American B-29 air raids, but an even stronger early memory is being hungry.

By the time I was old enough to understand what was going on, Japan was already involved with military actions and there was a food shortage. When World War II was at its peak for Japan, all the rice, wheat, and buckwheat went to the soldiers. The worst food shortage years for my family as well as all Japanese were 1943 through 1945. During the food shortages of these years, we ate mostly steamed *karaimo* 唐芋 (sweet potato). We put a slice of sweet potato in the middle of bread with butter, and then we would steam it. We also ate pickled daikkon and miso soup that contained daikkon, Irish potatoes, and fried tofu. When guests came, the fried tofu was of a higher quality, and my mother would also buy small fish from local fishermen to put into the soup. At the market, the small fish were dried on a straw mat and there would be flies all over them. We didn't consider flies to be dirty, but we did try to shoo them away.

Farmers sometimes secretly retained buckwheat to steam and eat, but it was illegal to have it. So, the retention and consumption of buckwheat became a hush-hush situation. But hiding buckwheat created a unity with neighbors. There would be ten to fifteen houses that shared buckwheat under the table. It they had extra, they shared. A person caught hoarding grain would be considered a traitor and would be arrested, jailed, and beaten. Further, their daughters would not be able to get married. So, an arrest would have had a tremendous impact on the entire family: all this risk was just to be able to eat. Under cover of night, people would dig a hole to bury and hide a large container of hoarded grains.

To get enough to eat, we all, even the children, had to be resourceful. When we were notified that there was no likelihood of bombs being dropped, I went to the creek to catch shrimp and eel. I knew secret places to catch shrimp, and eels would be hiding in small holes in the mud. The only net I had was a holey mosquito net my mother had tried to repair, but there were too many holes. So, I usually caught fish where the creek meets the ocean with my bare hands; I was very skillful at catching fish and seven-inch shrimp using this method. Because I was hungry, I became very adept at catching fish. At high tide, the ocean water goes into the creek, and at low tide, it's the opposite. There is a boundary where the creek water and ocean water mix, and this is where I found the shrimp. At that time, there were no chemicals in the water so there were many more fish, and they were much larger. I was a local hero in the fifth and sixth grades for being able to catch so many fish. We needed to help each other at this time, so I had no mentality to sell my catch. I gave many of the fish away to other families. The neighbor boy would catch shellfish and give them to my family. From April through October, the water was not too cold, so I could go fishing. In November, the baby octopi, which tasted better than the adults, were in the mud. The adult octopi were about one foot in length, and the babies were about five inches. There was deep mud, and I would slide my body over the mud as part of catching the fish: it was part play. Sometimes seashells cut my skin when I was sliding, but usually the salt water healed the wound very quickly; there were other times that the cuts became infected and were very itchy. I was also bitten, but I don't know what was doing the biting.

As children, we learned to catch shrimp and other sea life from our grandparents. The grandparents would usually do the catching, and the little girls and boys would hold the bucket to carry the shrimp. I also caught *asari* あさり (a saltwater sand clam species), but the most prized catch was eel. When I would take a catch home, my mother would call me a "good boy," and she would say that we would have a feast that night.

When I wasn't catching fish and shrimp or in the sand digging asari, I would be in the rice fields where there were many grasshoppers. I would catch them bare handed, too, and put them into a sack my mother had sewn together from scrap material. I had a bamboo pole with the sack at the end, and I would stuff the grasshoppers down a hollow stalk of bamboo. I would have a full sack by the time I went home. Sometimes the grasshoppers would try to climb back up the bamboo stalk, and I would have to tap them back down into the sack. My mother would steam and then dry them adding salt or soy sauce as the insect alone does not have much flavor. At a meal, we each got about a teacup full. In the beginning, it was difficult to accept eating them, but once you ate them, they tasted good, and they were naturally crunchy. Now, I would have a hard time to eat them. I didn't eat snake, but many people did.

At that time, there was not a single overweight person to be seen. Everyone moved briskly.

SCHOOL AND THE LESSONS OF WAR

Every aspect of our lives was colored by the war. Soldiers had begun occupying the school buildings one year before the war was over using them as barracks for sleeping and eating and the school grounds for training. So school was held in the Buddhist temple as it had been historically.

Each morning before going to the temple, we had an assembly at the schoolhouse. The principal stood on a stage, and we said the Pledge of Allegiance. He would then have the students look east toward Tokyo where the emperor resided and bow for thirty seconds. We couldn't perform these activities at our school temples because students had been divided into small groups and had to go to different temples, and the principal couldn't be at every site.

The few textbooks that we had were of low-quality paper with strings strung through holes instead of a proper binding. There was only one book for seven students; we rotated the books so that each student could take books home every seventh school day. I attended school every day, but there were not many academic subjects taught; we were mostly instructed through propaganda how to serve the country. There was a book that we were told was moral instruction but was, in reality, patriotic lessons. We were taught such things as the most superior human male was the German man, and the most superior human female was the Japanese woman.

School was deeply steeped in wartime activities. In case of an air raid, we students were taught to lie down between two rice fields in the concave area with our faces down. We were also taught to protect our ears and eyes by putting our thumbs into our ears and fingers over our eyes. My mother had made protective zabutons for all the family members. When they were used for ear protection from exploding bombs, they were called boku-zukin. In this case, we folded the thin zabutons in half and covered our heads to protect our ears. My mother had sewn a string into each zabuton so that we could tie it tightly to make a head covering. I carried my boku-zukin on my back twenty-four hours a day. My boku-zukin was not as fancy as the one pictured.

About one year before the war was over, there was a rumor circulating that American soldiers were going to enter Japan from Ariake Bay, a bay within a ten-minute walk from my home. So, the teachers taught students how to make bamboo spears (of a determined length) for self-defense, and at school, we practiced lunging. I recall being very excited about going to the temple for school, because I enjoyed spear practice so much. A teacher led the boy students with loud commands, and we would practice for more than an hour. We didn't associate the practice with stabbing a human being; spear lunging was just a game, but it was officially part of the curriculum. This was daily practice at school: in fact, during the war, more time was given to spear lunging types of exercises than studying.

A Child's Boku-zukin. http://wafuworks.blogspot.com/2010/08/childs-boku-zukin.html. Courtesy of Wafuworks.

When in a classroom setting, we continued with a daily routine. As the teacher walked into the classroom, a class president told students to stand, bow, and say in unison *ohayo-gozaimus* おはようございます (Good morning) to the teacher. After the first class, the students did not greet the teacher with a verbal greeting, but we would stand and wait until the teacher reached the desk and then bow when instructed to do so by the class president.

Our teachers were very conscientious and serious about their tasks, and they were highly respected. I think the teachers treated students as their own children, and that is why they became so upset if a student didn't live up to expectations. They would shout expressions like an upset parent: "How many times did I tell you?" If a teacher punished me by hitting me, I had been taught to say, "Thank you very much" to the teacher because I should be grateful that the teacher cared enough about my wellbeing to punish me. Even though I did not do really bad things, I was in a position to say, "Thank you very much" often. I was not a bully or a disruptive student, but because of my lack of interest and poor concentration, it was difficult for me to understand academic subjects. But I excelled in all areas of physical education. Once I changed into my PE uniform, I was in charge. My engine was running, and I was very happy. In my classmates' estimation, I ranked very high in running, jumping, and all sports. But at the same time, I was notorious for being poor in academic subjects. Once a year there was a national academic test, and I always scored below 50%.

My sisters were smart and did their homework: none of my siblings wanted our father to catch them not doing their homework. And since there was no television, most children did their homework. But even though I knew I should study, I would just go to bed and sleep without opening a book. When I woke up, I would worry that I had not done my homework, but I knew I would get help at school from two friends.

In class, we were seated boy, girl, boy, girl. I was seated between Kiyo-chan and Chie-chan, two of my female classmates. When they found out that I had not done my homework (and they always expected I hadn't), they would do it for me before school started. At exam time, Kiyo-chan would say to me, "Don't write your name," and then she took my exam, did it, and gave it back to me. She solved it very quickly (I was very slow) and gave it to me completed. She always intentionally missed problems. I asked her to give me one hundred percent just once, but she said the teacher would know that I was cheating if I were to get one hundred percent.

Sensei 先生 (teacher) Yamamura who taught English and PE, caught me cheating. He didn't announce it in class, but when I was outside, he said to me, "Kiyama, you did it again." I begged for pardon by asking him to forgive me and excuse me. He pardoned me, but he told me that studying is for my benefit, and the next time I should do my work myself. Sensei Yamamura's message was that he knew that I was good at sports, but that when I was no longer involved with sports, I needed to know as much as I could. Sensei Yamamura said that probably it would be better for him to hit me, but that he decided not to because I had an area in which I excelled: sports. He lectured me every time he caught me cheating, and that was often as I would be caught two or three times a week. He kindly patted me all the time during his lectures. Sensei Yamamura knew that I was getting help from the two girls, but he didn't say anything to them.

Thirty-five years after sixth grade, I talked on the phone with Kiyo-chan. She was a very good friend who gave me lots of homework support from sixth through ninth grades. I continue to feel very close to her and would like to hug her in gratitude, American style.

In school we were taught *Yamato-damashii* 大和魂 (Japanese spirit) and to offer *chugi* 忠義 (loyalty) to the country and to be prepared to die for the country. You were expected to offer your life for the country and if you died, you would become a *kami* 神 (spirit force or divinc force) and be worshipped at Yasukuni Shrine. These lessons taught us to admire *kami-kaze* 神風 *tokkotai* 特攻隊 (special attack unit) and the rituals surrounding them. Because a kami-kazi's body would probably not be found, he was to cut his fingernails and hair and leave them with his family. A pilot, who was preparing to become a kami-kazi, would be given a gift of ten cigarettes from the emperor. Before leaving for a final flight, the pilot was to smoke one of these cigarettes. My father's niece's husband expected he would not return from war and had prepared for death in this way before he left. When he was killed, a box was sent to the family and there were nine cigarettes from the emperor in it; the family added his hair and fingernails to the box. He had prepared well. When a family had a son returned to them as cremated ashes, people would say, "Your son has done well by serving the country."

WARNINGS, BITES, AND BURNS

We had advanced warning when bombers were coming. Radio NHK would announce how many hours and minutes before planes were to arrive based upon their location over an adjacent prefecture, but the nearer they came, we also knew they were coming simply by seeing and hearing them. A bell in a tall tower that was used in peacetime to indicate there was a fire, was frantically rung when enemy airplanes were en route. Over 100 B-29's would fly over, and they would be in the sky for two hours or more at a time. There was a military factory near my hometown, and a big fire could often be seen at a distance when the factory was bombed. Near the end of the war, Americans in the American version of the Japanese Zero loaded with machine guns would fly over during the day.

We painted all the walls in our houses black, and even in the summertime we were told not to wear white. At night, we looked for hills where we could dig holes for hiding. For two months before the end of the war, the bombs were dropped daily. My family and the neighbors dug a cave, and at one point, fifteen families shared the cave. As more people came to the cave for protection, we dug the cave larger. People couldn't work in the fields because of the enemy airplanes, so they would spend time digging the cave. If we were home when we became aware of approaching planes, we would head for the cave. The thinking was that if the cave were dug straight into the hill, and if a bomb landed on top of the hill, we would survive. The mornings after an air raid, the parents would count their children. They would clap with relief and joy when all were accounted for.

Even though we were almost starving, and we probably didn't have much blood, we were attacked in the cave by mosquitoes: they had to eat, too. There would be many mosquito bite bumps on our bodies. We were tired, hungry, trying to rest, and being mosquito bitten. We were in survival mode, and we didn't talk much about how we felt. There was little energy for feelings. Children slept. The adults might have their head drop with sleep, but then they would jerk awake. We were in a life and death situation, so the only help was mental strength: the desire to live.

The first time that I became aware of the war's ferocity involved my father's nieces, Tamiko-chun and Fuyuko-chun, my first cousins. Both were in their late teens, and they had lost their parents to American bombs. The girls needed to work, so they took jobs in a military factory. The factory they were working in was bombed, and they were badly burned. After being notified of their condition, my father left during the nighttime with straw mats in the rear of the car to get them. When he brought them to our house, he placed them in a small shed we had. The next day, I saw their bodies: they were at least ninety percent burned. My father suspended them from the ceiling with ropes covered with thick paper and lowered them so that only a small portion of their burned backs touched the floor. After a few days, liquid began oozing from the burned areas, and white worms were dropping from their legs. The shed smelled terrible. Neighbor women, who couldn't do farm work because of the bombing, came to help my family remove the worms from the girls' bodies using *hashi* 箸 (chopsticks). The girls felt very hot because of the burns, so my aunt would sit for hours fanning them. They said that the fanning was a great relief. The girls did not have the energy to scream; they were probably in shock, but they whimpered. My mother made a small hole in a bamboo pole with a funnel attached so that she could pour water into their mouths. She poured slowly so that they would not choke. She would feed them mashed sweet potato and *kabocha* 南瓜 (squash).

Six months after the factory bombing and the girls' burning, a blind woman who had learned herbal medicine, brought herbs and white paper to the shed where they lay. She said that it was important not to use scissors to cut the paper: it had to be torn. She applied herbal medicine to my father's nieces' entire bodies and then covered the medicine with the torn white paper. At the borders where the paper patches touched, the body liquid continued to flow. The blind woman later died without revealing what herbs she used, but the girls survived, and their skin showed no evidence of having been burned. In 2015, they were still living: Tamiko-chun was eighty years old, and Fuyuko-chun was eighty-three years old.

NAGASAKI: AN UNUTTERABLE END
AUGUST 9, 1945

My life had been normal until the Americans entered the war.

Near the end of the war there were air raids every day, and military factories about forty minutes by bicycle from my house were the main targets of the American B-29's. The B-29's bombed factories at night, but during the day, smaller American airplanes would fly over my town. If the pilots saw human movement on the ground, they swooped down and used machine guns to shoot people. I did not have any friends who were killed by these attacks, but I knew people who died in them. If someone were shot, no one went to help the person until nighttime for fear of being shot themselves.

School was cancelled completely during this period of daily air raids, so I had time to go fishing every day with my aunt, Asae, my mother's younger sister. She lived with us after her husband, with whom she had only spent four hours of marriage before his departure to the war, had been killed in battle. Before this fishing outing with my aunt on August 9, 1945, there had been many consecutive days that bombs were dropped. She and I knew there was a chance we could be bombed or shot while fishing, but we were hungry.

On Thursday August 9, 1945, my aunt and I were the only people fishing that day, and we were fishing for *haze* ハゼ (goby) and halibut, and we caught many fish! It was a beautiful, bright, and sunny day with perfectly clear skies. In fact, my aunt commented about it being such a clear day that we could see a train on the other side of Nagasaki Bay, a forty-minute train ride to Nagasaki. Nagasaki was of interest to the United States militarily because it was a shipbuilding center.

Around 11:00 a.m., my aunt and I were seated on the dirt bank fishing. I was fishing with a bamboo rod that I would pull up and down in a slow rhythm to keep the bait moving. Certainly, there was no rain on that clear day, but all of a sudden we saw lightning in the sky: it was not like any lightning either my aunt or I had ever seen. It was wide and thick but without sound, an unsettling and unnatural event. We wondered aloud why there was lightning when there were no clouds, but after two or three minutes, a huge cloud appeared. First, the cloud went straight up and then it began to spread out becoming thicker and thicker creating a peculiar shape. We had seen lots of bombings and the subsequent smoke, and at night we had seen what looked like falling fire from hundreds of B-29's, but my aunt said this was different from what we had witnessed before. I wanted to continue fishing, but she pulled me by my arm and insisted that it was time to go home. I wasn't afraid—I was hungry, but my aunt had an uneasy feeling and said, "Today is different."

So, I had no choice, and we went home. Since there had been no sound, we could only tell people what we had seen. The people we told wanted to confirm what we reported, but they were afraid to go outside because they might be shot. We were not able to tell many people as we, too, were afraid to go out.

Everyone knew about the Hiroshima atomic bombing on August 6, 1945, but since there were no televisions, we had not seen the images of the bombing or the subsequent cloud, but we had heard about it over the radio. We heard on the radio the bomb that fell on Hiroshima was the size of a matchbox, but since we did not know the physics, it was beyond our common sense. And anyway, by this point, we did not really trust information on the radio.

I did not know that what my aunt and I had seen had been the Nagasaki atomic bomb until the next day when I listened to the radio. And later, when the emperor spoke on August 15, 1945, he confirmed that Nagasaki had been bombed with an atomic bomb.

END OF WAR, AUGUST 15, 1945

I was almost nine years old at the end of the war.

On August 14, 1945, people were told they should listen to the radio at eight o'clock the following morning: the emperor was to

My Aunt Asae, left, with whom I witnessed the Nagasaki bomb explosion, and my mother, right.

speak. I am not too sure, but probably many people expected the radio speech would be an announcement of surrender. Five or six minutes before 8:00 a.m., my father told everyone to sit down; his behavior was calmer than usual. We all sat in *seiza* facing the radio, and we were all dead serious. My father sat in the middle of the front row: I was next to him, and all my brothers were in the front row. The girls and my mother sat behind us. It was six days after the Nagasaki bomb had been dropped. We had not talked about the Hiroshima bomb because it would have been admitting defeat, and no one used the word defeat because people would have said you are not a patriot, or you were not Japanese.

My father sternly said, "Quiet!" And everyone listened. The NHK presenter announced there would be a pronouncement by the emperor. At exactly 8:00 a.m., the emperor began to talk and continued for about five minutes. There was lots of static on the radio that had to be controlled. I can still recall the way the radio sounded. The emperor's voice rolled like a wave up and down; the radio condition made his voice strong then soft, strong, soft. I remember he said there would be an unconditional surrender. He never used the word defeat, but he did use the word surrender. My father began to cry, and because he cried, all the children and my mother cried. The small children didn't know why they were crying, but they cried.

My father stood up but didn't go any place, and since the announcement had been made before breakfast, when it was over, my mother served my father green tea. At the very moment she was serving him tea, the oldest daughter of my father's friend came running into our house and told my father in a tremulous voice that her father was dying. My father took off running to his friend's house just five houses away, and I followed. He dashed into the house; I was right behind him. I saw my father's friend but didn't understand what was going on until I saw his intestines. It had taken about thirty seconds to register what was happening. My father's face was utter shock. When we arrived, his friend was sitting in seiza and had already cut his abdomen: the cut from the *tanto* 短刀 (short sword) he had used was more than one foot long. Steam was coming out of the wound, but there was little blood. The intestines appeared to be inside a thin sack, and my father's friend was holding his own intestines. His sword was on the floor in front of him. My father was holding his friend's shoulder and gently touching him asking, "Are you okay?" Meanwhile, his friend turned white, then a light purple, and then he fell over. He was alive, but he could only nod. Later, I thought that the nod was a message saying that he would die first before my father committed *seppuku* (ritualistic suicide through disembowelment). We were all in shock. His wife was in a different room crying a sort of shock crying that I had never heard before or since.

While we were still at my father's friend's house, the son of another friend of my father's dashed into the house in great distress shouting that his father desperately needed help. When we reached his house, my father's friend was dead and had fallen to the floor. He had made a *komo* 薦 (straw mat) on which he had performed formal *seppuku* 切腹. My father lifted him as his trembling wife came out with a cup of water for her husband, but my father said it was too late. She lost her balance and tried to go deeper into the house, but she couldn't walk straight, and she fell against a door—she couldn't move forward. Her daughter helped her.

These two ritual suicides took place within less than one hour of each other, and they remain vivid in my mind. I had been told the meaning of seppuku, but this was the first time to see the real thing. Even though I had been told why they had done this, I was puzzled.

Walking home, my father was surprisingly calm. I remember the odd feeling when we opened the door to our house, and the birds that nested in our foyer flew out the door as they always had as if nothing had happened. As soon as we entered the house through the foyer, my father began frantically searching for something in various places. I didn't know what he was looking for, but he kept searching without saying a word. He was pale and had a determined look on his face.

My father sat in the sunroom without speaking, but soon he went back and rechecked all the places he had checked earlier. Later I learned that my mother and my oldest sister had known what my father was looking for, but I continued in the dark. My mother had sensed the war would not last much longer, and she knew her husband: she decided to bury his sword. I later learned that about one month before the emperor's announcement, my mother buried my father's sword. My mother and father had seven children to support; there were many of us depending upon his living. Not until maybe a year later, did I figure out that he had been hunting for his sword. There is no question that my father would have committed seppuku. His face was completely different from his normal face, and he was in shock over having lost his friends. He felt that if he did not commit suicide, that he was not a genuine Japanese, and that his friends who had committed suicide were. He felt that his country came first, and if the country died, he would, too. My mother had prevented him from committing seppuku, but my father didn't smile for one year after the end of WWII.

When my life was at its hardest, I thought maybe I should die, and I even dreamed about the two incidents of seppuku I had witnessed and my father's desire to commit seppuku. I thought that if you work so hard that you might die but are prepared for death, then you can work much harder. If you are willing to give up your life, you can accomplish much more. My emotional strength grew very fast when I realized this.

After the War

UNSCATHED BY WAR BUT CHANGED BY BARBERS

I was not permanently traumatized by the war, but immediately after the war, I had nightmares of the bombings. These nightmares lasted until I began judo at thirteen years old. But a child's fear is different from an adult's: I believe that my parents had an intense fear, but as a child, I didn't interpret the war events as dangerous in the same deep and lasting way. We children didn't know how to interpret the bombings. I was primarily hungry. After all, I was with my parents. Maybe it was a false sense of security, but we expected our parents to take care of us. And they did the best they could.

After the war, as before and during, some things remained the same, giving us some sense of normalcy. Our hair was one of the areas that remained constant. The boys all had the same haircut style: cut one-fourth of an inch long. In fact, no one grew hair any longer than that until quite some time after WWII. My father cut the boys' hair using a set of manual clippers, but he didn't have a tool to shave around our ears. We were not allowed to use oil on our hair, but our hair was so short, it didn't make any difference. My sisters helped each other put their hair up, and sometimes they heated a tool like a curling iron and made curls. They always had bangs, and they were allowed to grow their hair but only to their shoulders.

When I was older, I wanted to go to the barber to get a professional haircut, but customarily, people only went to a barber if they were going on a job interview. The barbers used electric clippers and shaved neatly around the ears, which my father could not do. My father had forbidden me to go to the barber, but on the sly, my mother gave me money to go. The first time I went, I was wearing dirty clothes, and the barber refused to cut my hair. I was told to come back after I changed into clean clothes. I cleaned up and returned, and when I went home from the barber with my hair cut and neatly shaven around my ears, my mother was quite impressed; it would have cost extra to have had my face shaved, so I only had them shave around my ears. She understood that I had a girl I liked. I was afraid that my father would be angry about the forbidden haircut, so I put a towel over my head to hide the freshly barbered hair. My father saw the towel, and suspecting something, he roughly jerked it off. He shouted that I was not old enough to go to a barbershop, and that I was just a child and didn't deserve to go.

The result of the professional barbers was clearly visible, and that is why I paid to go to the barber. I thought girls would pay more attention to me. And after I met my childhood sweetheart, Chieko, I went to the barber's shop regularly.

ON JAPANESE SOIL: AMERICAN SOLDIERS

What was not familiar after the war was the presence of the American soldiers.

When the American soldiers came on the ground as the winners, their arrival was interpreted as an invasion. We thought we would be killed, but to our surprise, the soldiers didn't act aggressively. In fact, the soldiers would be driving in their ten-wheeled trucks, and when they saw us children, they would stop and throw butterscotch-drops, red-stripped peppermint candy wrapped in cellophane paper, and Hershey's bite-sized candy to us. When the soldiers stopped in their trucks, we children hurriedly ran to get the treats and more hurriedly withdrew because we thought the candy was bait to draw us in to be shot. Some of the chocolate had white letters written on it, but we couldn't read what they said. The soldiers also gave us *Dentyne* and *Spearmint* chewing gum. The gum was so sweet that I ate it, and I could see it in my bowel movements. Later I was told not eat it.

During this time, parents could not afford to give children candy; later I understood that giving candy was a way for the soldiers to catch the children's hearts and trust. The rapport between the children and soldiers was sweet, and the children ultimately interpreted it as a positive relationship. The soldiers' guns caused me to be afraid, but with time, I began to think of the Americans as kind. After three or four months, I was sure the soldiers would not kill me, but my father was prideful and told us not to eat the American candy. As long as my father was not around, my mother would eat the candy, too. She really enjoyed it and said that American candy was good. The sugar tasted extremely sweet after having only solid black sugar and grass roots for years, so it was a race by the children to get the candy. We would gather as much as we could and put it in our shirts. The soldiers communicated with lots of smiles, and they would use a few Japanese expressions with us such as *Ohayo gozaimasu* おはようございます (Good Morning), *genki?* 元気 (How are you?), or *hai* はい (yes). I quickly came to learn two American expressions that the soldiers used frequently: "Thank you" and "Okay." The soldiers were very friendly, and for about one year, they encouraged us children to come for the treats that they would distribute.

These soldiers were the first humans for me to see with such a different appearance from Japanese: they had different hair color and texture, they were physically large, and their eye color was different. I saw blue eyes for the first time and was afraid to look into their eyes. Initially I was also afraid to shake hands: the soldiers would extend their hands to shake, but I would refuse. The soldiers were so toweringly tall, and they would tease us by jumping at us, but they knew that we enjoyed it.

Almost all the children who got candy from the soldiers were boys. A few tomboys were brave enough to take candy directly from the soldiers, but most of the girls were afraid and would just watch from a distance. The boys would share with the girls, and I was one of the most generous boys. I liked being a boss, so I was willing to generously share with the girls, and of course, they liked me very much. I was very quiet in school, but I was good at getting candy, and it was my pride that I could get more candy than the other boys.

I, HUNTING DOG

One day, a soldier picked me up and placed me in the truck. I thought I was being kidnapped, but he opened the candy box and let me take as much as I wanted. I forgot all about being kidnapped. After that, I requested to be taken directly to the box. Before the war, it was understood and accepted that all older people had authority, and young people had to be polite to them. But the American soldiers, all of whom were older, had no authoritative attitude toward the children. Once I got used to the social exchange, it was all very pleasurable.

At this time in Japan, smiling and joking around were not welcome as they were considered a sign of weakness and insincerity. Therefore, I could not be frisky at home, but when I was with the American soldiers, I would go crazy acting happily. Every day after school I would look for the trucks filled with American soldiers, and I would spend between thirty minutes to an hour with them.

Many times, the soldiers would stop their jeeps and ask me to get in. Even though I hesitated at first, I did get in, and through gestures, they let me know that they wanted to go hunting. I directed them to the beach where there were ducks, and they would shoot them for sport. I was the dog in this hunting expedition. The ducks that were shot might land in the river, and I would swim to get them. The soldiers were delighted and laughed a great deal to see me collect the birds: I was an entertainment monkey for them. After I caught the ducks, the soldiers would pick me up, soaking wet, and give me a hug. I realized that was the American way to say, "thank you." I understood from their hugs that they were happy, and that I had done a good job. They would give me the ducks they shot plus candy. I knew how to lace the ducks onto a rope, and with great pride, I would carry them home. My father knew how to prepare duck, and he very quickly made duck soup. It was a feast.

Japanese don't hunt or eat frogs, but the soldiers gave me the hint that they wanted to hunt them. I didn't know how to catch frogs, but

I knew that frogs tend to jump on red material. So, I covered three hooks with red material and shined a light on it. A bullfrog jumped on it, and I caught the frog. The soldiers liked to eat frog meat, and they gave me a taste of it: it was delicious. They also gave me a handful of coins that may still be somewhere in my family's former house.

We children played games with the soldiers, which strengthened our trust in them. The soldiers would hold sumo matches with us children and would put out piles of candy as prizes. I would try very hard to win, and I would make faces of exertion to show how hard I was trying. The soldiers intentionally lost so that the children would get the candy. This was just another way for the soldiers to show that they were not there to kill us but rather to gain our trust. Of course, I only realized all this much later when I looked back on those days. I think that if one country defeats another, the winner must do its best to make peace. Peace is not easy.

Soldiers were getting close to the Japanese people in other ways. I knew a very poor family whose daughter disappeared for a time from the village, but when she returned at New Years, she came with many nice clothes and leather high heels. I found out later she was working as a prostitute at a bar for American soldiers. She came back rich and helped her family. She was not the only girl who left and returned wearing fancy clothing, and we children were in awe of them. They got lots of attention even though parents told their children not to look at them. When we asked why we should not look at them, they wouldn't answer. Regardless, we were aware that their condition was very much changed: they left very poor, but after six months, they came back much better off. The parents tried to keep it a secret that their daughters were prostitutes, but all the adults knew that the neighbor girls had been able to get all these fancy clothes because they had been a prostitute. The children thought that they had become movie stars.

At that time, many of the American teenaged soldiers fell in love with the prostitutes. Japanese women in those days were expected to serve men, so prostitutes were serving in the same manner they were expected to serve at home. American soldiers were astonished at the subservience of the prostitutes and didn't want to let them go. So, they proposed marriage. In reality, when the married women came to the United States, they would become strong-minded and would tell their husbands what to do. At one time, there were about eight hundred of these women who had been prostitutes and married American soldiers living not far from my current home in the United States. By now, they are dead or very old.

NIGHT SOIL—AN ACCIDENT

American soldiers would not eat Japanese vegetables because they had been grown with night soil (human excrement used as fertilizer). After WWII, some farmers had a contract with the military, but the military insisted that the farmers not use night soil. That was the beginning of chemical fertilizer usage in Japan.

Our toilets before, during, and for some time after WWII, were not flush toilets. We had an "outhouse within the house" style toilet, a *kumitori benjo* 汲み取り便所 (a toilet for night soil collection). For my family, an extra-large hole was dug because we had many people. As one of seven children, I had no time to read a book in the bathroom. We didn't have toilet paper, so my mother would cut newspaper into different sizes and place it beside the toilet. When the newspaper stopped being delivered during the war, the boys used a rope made of the stalk of rice called *nawa* 縄 to wipe; my mother washed it between uses. We moved it front to back, and it was very painful.

The toilet had an outside access so that farmers could gather the human waste easily to fertilize their gardens. The farmers did not pay the house owner for the night soil they carried away, but to show their appreciation, they would share some of their first crops with contributors. The farmers collected the night soil in a beautifully made big wooden scoop basket, a *koetago* 肥たご. The wooden koetago had a rope and two loops through which a wooden bar was placed. It was called a "six-foot bar," and it had a hook so that the koetago wouldn't slip. It was designed for carrying a heavy load. Human waste along with left over vegetables, fish, and chicken was carried to a pond-like hole beside a garden or field and composted there. The waste would be dumped there and would age for about six months to a year. It smelled horrible, and if you needed to pass by this area, you would hold your nose and run very fast. After six months, the smell diminished.

When I was in seventh grade, my father thought that carrying human waste to the gardens and fields would be a good experience for me. My father said that you can better appreciate the food you eat that the farmer grows if you know what he must do. My father's lesson was that you should understand the hard job the farmer has before you enjoy the delicious results of rice and vegetables. So, I would collect our waste and carry it to the fields and gardens. The contents of the bucket were more liquid than solid, so unless you walked very steadily with a particular rhythm on the unpaved and bumpy road, the liquid would shift.

One day as I was carrying the waste, a public bus came by, and I was afraid of being spotted by my friends doing such dirty and humiliating work; as I tried to avoid the embarrassment of being seen by the people on the bus, the bar began to swing. I lost my coolness and spilled the entire bucket in the middle of the street! Then, as if that weren't embarrassing enough, I fell in the mess face first. The people on the bus saw what had happened and were laughing and clapping.

I smelled so bad that I couldn't go home, and since we didn't have outside hoses at that time, I found a small creek and rinsed off. My father said that I still stank, and he told me to wash with soap. He prepared clean water and a bamboo broom and swept the spilled human waste that was on the street into a ditch. Maggots, which eat the bacteria in the night soil and eventually leave a very nice fertilizer, were all over the street from the spill.

I successfully carried the waste one more time after the spill, but that was the last time.

My family taught that at school you learn school subjects, but at home, you must learn life and spiritual lessons. This type of education is missing today. The family structure today is completely different from the structure I was raised in, and the lack of proper home education is one of the explanations for many of society's current problems.

JUDO ("SHUT UP")

My father had plans for each of his children.

For me, when I was thirteen years old and the right age to begin judo, my father decided to enroll me in the Takenouchi Judo School.

The dojo was in the *Komin-kan* 公民館 (cultural center) and since the town sponsored the building in which the dojo was located, the fee was very little.

The official reason for teaching judo at that time was to keep young people out of trouble and to teach moral lessons through judo. My father's reason, however, was that I must learn judo because I was not good at academic subjects. He later told me that he had insisted I go to the dojo because he believed I needed to get a black belt to be taken seriously in society. At the time, a black belt was highly respected. In my prefecture, Kumamoto, people were famous for being highly skilled in sports, and traditional *budo* 武道 (the way of samurai) was encouraged, so it was natural that my father would want me to participate in sports.

The head of the Takenouchi School dojo was Sensei Tateyama, but he was too old to teach because he could not demonstrate. So, my actual and first judo instructor, Seigo Kitano, had been a navy instructor, and he was about forty-five years old. I was afraid of him because he had a stern expression; he never smiled. In fact, those first three years, my teacher never laughed or smiled. If I made a mistake, he would shout, "How many times did I tell you!" I wanted to cry, but if I had cried, he would have told my father, and my father would have hit me. To avoid crying, I tried to make my face tight by clenching my teeth. If my mother had been there, I would have cried, but if I had, the others would have called me a sissy. The one time crying is acceptable, however, is if you win at a tournament. Even the instructors cry when their students win.

The first three years of judo were so painful that I always wanted to quit. I was thirteen, fourteen, and fifteen years old, and my body and joints were still growing; most of the other students were eighteen or nineteen. I complained to my father that I didn't want to go to the dojo. So, he made my attendance conditional: if I didn't go to the dojo, I couldn't have dinner. I questioned whether I was being taught judo, because I knew pain was not associated with judo, so many times I asked my instructor whether what we were practicing was really judo. Usually I was told, "Shut up. It's not polite to ask questions." "This is classical judo," my instructor said. I knew I should not question authority, but my question was natural because judo is known for throwing techniques not pain. But in fact, it was not judo; it was *jujitsu* 柔術 (an older martial art from which judo derived), which does have painful techniques: in judo, the *gi* 衣 (clothing) is grabbed, but in jujitsu, skin is grabbed causing a great deal of pain. My father thought that he had taken me to learn judo, and he wasn't completely wrong, because judo comes from jujitsu. Also, he was not familiar with the distinction between jujitsu and judo because he had never practiced either of them; he had only practiced sumo. When I attended the Takenouchi School, jujitsu and judo were blended because judo was not yet recognized as an Olympic sport, and the distinction between the two was not clear. I suffered those three years practicing jujitsu, but now I believe it was beneficial.

Sensei Kitano was like a devil at the dojo, but at parties, he was a nice man. This was typical of the judo teacher to be stern at the dojo and friendly outside. But he encouraged me to continue with judo. He had four children of his own who were a little older than I: one girl and three boys, but none of them did judo.

After two years and ten months of my jujitsu training, a second instructor, Susumau Takahashi, joined our dojo. He was also from the navy, and so we had two people teaching who were retired navy instructors. Takahashi Sensei was seven years younger than Kitano Sensei. They had not known each other until Takahashi began teaching, but they taught well together.

I continued to complain to my father because practice at the dojo was so painful, but he insisted that I continue because he said working through the pain would teach me perseverance. My father said that a Japanese man had to be a *Kyushu-danji* 九州男児 (a man of Kyushu spirit), and the expression has a bit of a macho meaning. This pressure to be manly is especially true for Kyushu men.

Training

I went to judo five or six nights a week from 7:00 p.m. to 10:00 p.m. I had a light meal before judo, but after our severe training, we judoists were very hungry and would stop at a noodle shop for *udon* うどん (wheat noodles) or *soba* そば (buckwheat noodles). Only four or five people would go because many didn't have enough money; those who did not join us went home directly and ate leftovers from supper. Sometimes we would all pitch in to pay for someone who couldn't afford to buy noodles.

When I started judo, I was not a well-developed guy, not particularly muscular. But after three years, I had built up a great deal of muscle.

Every night I did one hundred judo push-ups. I also frog jumped across eighty mats three times (about ten minutes), but I didn't do weightlifting until I was about twenty years old. After I was sixteen years old, I also went up the Buddhist temple steps (forty-two steps) with my arms behind my back and in a squatting position: up and down. I did three rounds of forty-two steps up and forty-two steps down. I would go step by step, but it didn't take long. During the four months of winter, we judoists ran on the beach with no shoes for a minimum of one hour and a maximum of two or three hours. We had rigorous training because we were no longer only improving ourselves: we were competing. When I was ages thirteen through fifteen, I did not go to the Tamana-shi martial arts building, a larger dojo, because I was afraid. But from age sixteen, once or twice a week three of us would take a forty-five-minute bicycle ride to the larger dojo to get better training rather than just being comfortable in our home dojo.

A more passive form of training at that time was to allow yourself to be choked out. My instructor usually waited six months but within the first year, he had everyone experience being choked until passed out or at least choked to the point of passing out. He thought it was important for all of us to experience how it felt to pass out from being choked. One method of choking is through compression of the windpipe, and the other way is to stop the blood from going to the brain. Initially, when being choked out, the person feels a tight and uncomfortable force followed by a feeling of going a long distance: then suddenly, nothing. After a student passed out, the sensei tried to revive him by slapping his face. Slapping showed how deeply unconscious the student was. If he were not successful in bringing the student back to consciousness through slapping, the teacher approached from behind and put his knee in the middle of the backbone and his two arms under the student's arms. Then he pulled on the student's arms and at the same time pushed his knee into the student's back. The unconscious person's chest was pushed out, and he began to breathe. Upon becoming conscious, some people threw up.

I have experienced being choked out and have watched others pass out. In fact, I have been unconscious about seven times. When my teacher noticed I was not paying attention, he would choke me

Weightlifting. I was twenty-one years old and was standing in front of my house.

until I passed out. After I revived, I was very well focused. The teacher was careful with beginners, however. He knew I was in good shape, so he didn't hesitate to choke me out. My teacher used this technique as a threat to students who were not working hard enough, but his threat caused several people to quit. Instructors considered choking fundamental education at that time. Students who survived this hardship got the glory and respect of the black belt. (Today I don't use the choking technique in my instruction at all even though it is not illegal, and even though I have never heard of anyone dying from being choked. Since choking is not taught now, the students don't know how to do it or how to escape from it.)

During the coldest time of the year, we had a special winter condensed training called *Kangeiko* 寒稽古, which started between January 5 and January 10. On the fifteenth day, we took *mochi* 餅 (rice cake from made from glutinous rice) to the miniature dojo Shinto shrine where we had placed it earlier and put it in a big pot with sweet *azuki* あずき (red mung bean) and heated it. I would eat at least eleven bowls of the sweet mochi.

Judo Gi 柔道衣 *(Judo uniform)*

Originally, the practice of judo was for self-improvement not for winning a competition, and the white color of the judo gi was a symbol of purity, fairness, and cleanliness. We were allowed to fold the gi on the mat and then put it over our arm, but after it had been folded, it was not to be on the mat. The girls were nuts about a judoist carrying his folded gi over his arm.

My home dojo had forty or fifty people, and during the summertime we met every day: there was a powerful sweat smell throughout the dojo. With time, when we were further from the poverty of the war, everyone was expected to have a minimum of two judo gis because during the rainy season, the gis would not dry completely, and even though we washed them, the gis became smellier and smellier. Some of the judoists still couldn't afford two gis, so upon entering the dojo, the smell of sweat and mold was overwhelming. The gis smelled so bad that bad breath appeared mild. Part of the training, however, was to develop mental strength to overcome this type of unpleasantness, and besides, after ten or fifteen minutes, we didn't notice the smell. Complaining about smells is a luxury today. It was secondary then, and we grew stronger.

When we finished practice, our gis were completely soaked with perspiration, but as part of our training, we were not allowed to drink water during practice. Now I wonder whether people lack perseverance in judo because they drink water during practice, but medically, I accept the concern over dehydration. After finishing practice, we went to a water pump and drank from our hands. We also tried to make our body wet by using the pumped water as a shower splashing it on our chests. The younger students pumped the water, and the elder students got wet.

When I only had one judo gi, I used bar soap to scrub it, but then I would put it in a tub of cold water and stomp on it because it still smelled. The gi was still quite damp when I used it the next night. In the winter, I only washed the gi every two or three weeks, and I washed it quickly; everyone smelled anyway. Before a tournament, however, we had to thoroughly wash the gis. During a tournament, if the gi were not washed properly, the judge would score the judoist lower.

Under the gi, we wore fresh underwear every day. We wore *fundoshi* 褌通, the samurai style underpants: we didn't have boxers or briefs. My younger brother, Futoru, wore a red fundoshi to protect himself from jock rot. I wore the red one, too, until I came to the United States; I wear briefs now. The old style is very airy, but I didn't want to be laughed at, so I quit wearing the fundoshi. I thought they were too old-fashioned, and I said goodbye to the old-style underpants. My grandfather said that a six-foot fundoshi can be unfurled when crossing a body of water as protection against sharks as they won't attack anything longer than their height. You just untie it and let it furl out. The fundoshi is very firm in the genital area but airy and comfortable.

When I was awarded *shodan* 初段 (first degree) in 1952, there were no colored belts: I went straight from white to black. After WWII, judo became a sport, so the brown belt was introduced into Japan. Colorful belts began in the United States or Europe because for the teacher, judo was a business. The concept of many-colored belts: yellow, blue, orange, green, and purple, was a money-making scheme, and while a few places in Japan use them, most don't. The first-time colored belts were officially seen was in the 1964 Tokyo Olympics. Judo became a sport during the Tokyo Olympics, 1964, and the Kodokan style of judo, my style, was the international style. (European countries were asking for kendo to become an Olympic sport, but the Kendo Federation was against winning as a goal as it would be if it were an Olympic sport.) For international judo games in Japan, both players wear white judo gis, but outside Japan, they wear blue and white. Two colors make it easier for judges to determine calls, but as a traditionalist, I believe both gis should be white.

Policemen had training in the same dojo that I did so we came to recognize each other. Once I was riding my bicycle without a headlight which was against the law. In fact, a person could get a ticket for failing to have a headlight. There was a policeman standing on a corner who stopped me, and I thought I was going to get a ticket, but because I was in my judo gi, he let me go. That was a meaningful event because a policeman was the authority, and he had showed respect over law toward a fellow judoist.

The Black Belt

During my first three years of practice, I had no matches. When my teacher thought I was ready to compete for a black belt, I went to the main dojo where all the candidates for a black belt gathered. The opportunity was available only once a year. The candidates were divided into random groups of six; they were not grouped according to weight. To earn a black belt, I needed to beat the other five people in my group. Four groups would be on the mat at one time, and after they finished, another four groups began. I failed to get the black belt the first two years: the first year I won two matches, lost two, and had one draw; the second year, I won three, and lost two. When candidates in the first group finished, they could leave, but the second year, I stayed and watched because I knew I might meet these people again. I had to travel one hour from home to Kumamoto City; I had left home at 6:00 a.m. and didn't return until 9:00 p.m.

When I lost, I told my father I had not gotten the black belt, and he said it was because I lacked effort. My mother wouldn't contradict my father, but later she called me to her and said not to worry about it, that I would do well later. If my father had heard her talking so sweetly, he would have said that she shouldn't speak sweetly to me after I lost.

In 1952, my third attempt, I beat five people. For the winners, a qualifying exam was held in the afternoon. For the qualifying exam, I had to perform *nage-no-kata* 投の形 (formal throwing forms). This portion was divided into three categories: hand, hip, and leg skills. Following the nageno-kata exam was a written exam. All exams were given on the same day, and I passed easily. The written exam, twenty questions, had to be completed within one hour. There are people who fail the kata part; they must wait another year to try again, but they didn't have to fight the five again. No one fails the written part. After winning five matches and passing the qualifying exam, I was told I had gotten the black belt: my teacher bowed to me. My teacher didn't offer any encouraging words: he just said that I now understood my real ability. I passed the test when I was seventeen years old, but the certificate arrived after my eighteenth birthday. A formal certificate came six months later from the Kodokai, and my certificate number is: 14,014.

Most people take more than three attempts to earn a black belt. I was just seventeen years old and had gotten the black belt after three attempts, so I thought I was doing very well. The dojo against which we were competing had a high level of judoists, and many of these judoists were trying for the third or fourth time to get a black belt. After five years of practicing, I began to see the benefit of perseverance, and I finally agreed that it had been a great idea to suffer through the training. One of the benefits of the perseverance was the attention I got from girls because I had a black belt. That part I really enjoyed!

Americans often hug to show pleasure after someone they care about has success. This is not a Japanese custom. My sensei had been very severe, but when I finally won the black belt, he cried. Even on that occasion, I tried not to cry. At home, my father prepared a celebratory tai fish, and my mother made a thankful gesture and a prayer. After the prayer, she cried, bowed, and clapped. Being an intelligent woman and very skilled at manipulating her children, she took full advantage of my judo promotion; I wasn't good at waking up, so she said that a guy with a black belt should be able to get up on his own. My brothers were impressed and feared my strength. My older sister patted me, and everyone congratulated me. My stock went up, and my authority increased. After getting the black belt, my brothers and sisters treated me with respect, and I wasn't as approachable as I used to be. I had been used to teasing and playing with them, but now I had to show pride and couldn't act simply as a sibling any longer. I had to behave more respectably, and I couldn't play any more with my siblings. Even my father totally changed his attitude toward me. He told me that since I was now a black belt and no longer a white belt, I needed to be more mature and had to control myself. I couldn't be silly. When no family members or other adults were around, however, I reverted to talking about girls and all the other less serious topics in life.

My experience in the dojo was affected by having gotten the black belt, too, not just at home. After getting the black belt and returning to my dojo, the white belts who had failed to get a black belt, were eager to challenge me. My pride would not allow me to be thrown by them. So, at the dojo I was treated differently, too, but after practice was over, we all went back to normal.

A judo rule at the time was that high school students could not earn beyond a second-degree black belt, but two did: Haruo Imamura and Saburo Matsushita. (Imamura died 9/19/17 from colon cancer.) They both earned sandan: third degree while they were still in high school. Haruo Imamura was three years older than I and was a better judoist. He practiced at his high school and at the *budokan* 武道館 (martial arts hall). Three other judoists and I went to watch him practice at a judo dojo in the Tamana-city's budokan. We had to ride bikes for forty-five minutes one-way to get there, but it was worth it because the level of judo at this dojo was very high. We didn't go inside to watch, but we put our bicycles at the windows and stood on the bicycles and watched through the window. Imamura had been in Manchuria

(Northeast China) for about twelve years, but he returned to Japan after WWII. He was a high school champion at that time, and he was well known all over Japan for his judo ability. Imamura was a taller and bigger man than I, and while I never competed in a match with him, he and I practiced together. The best that I could do was to make Imamura lose his balance, and we would both fall. I never beat him.

A Dangling Eyeball
Once a year, a high-ranking policeman came to the main judo dojo to give a demonstration, and many clubs would attend. A well-built policeman, Tomita, who was about six or seven years older than I, was practicing with one of the students. My friend, Mr. Sakai, was also practicing with another student. Sakai was thrown, and when he was turning, his heel swung in the air and hit the policeman's left eye. His eyeball popped out, and I saw it hanging; it dropped about three inches down his face, still connected by what looked like a yellow straight cord, like a mixture of a large nerve and small wires and strings. We used gauze to cover his left eye, and a *judo obi* 帯 (belt) to hold the gauze over the eye. There was a great deal of blood as if it were flowing from a spring, pulsating, but it eventually stopped. I was shocked, scared, and worried, and so were the eighty people who were there, and for about ten or twenty seconds, there was complete silence. There was no emergency number or ambulance at that time, so we removed the shoji and used it as a stretcher. It took eight of us (because Tomita was a big man we had to take turns as carriers) about twenty-five minutes, jogging, to transport him to the hospital, and all the time, the policeman was holding his own eye with the gauze. Mr. Sakai, who had kicked him, kept saying, "*Gomen-nasai, Gomen-nasai,*" ごめんなさい (I am sorry), but the policeman said not to worry that he would not die. Those who did not go to the hospital continued practicing judo.

Japanese men should not admit to being in pain or being frightened, and Tomita never complained: the doctors cut the nerves and gave him a glass eye. He had been the head of a special police force, but after the accident he was given a desk job. Ultimately, he retired from the police force and served as the Commissioner of Welfare. But he was able to continue judo. After he recovered from the judo accident, he talked about the accident saying that he had been beyond pain. At this time, I had already earned a black belt and seeing such a horrifying accident did not frighten me enough to discontinue judo.

I have never had such a serious injury as Tomita had, but I broke my knee many times in judo. In some ways I was lucky to break my knee because Chieko, the girl I liked, came with candy four times to visit me. She came whenever I was injured: she couldn't admit why she was coming to my house because it would have been too embarrassing, so she said she had come to play with my younger sister. Each time Chieko came to visit, my mother told me that she was a good girl, and that I should make her mine. My father, on the other hand, reminded me that I should never touch a girl unless I could support her and planned to marry her.

In Japan, I participated in judo for ten years from age thirteen until I left Japan in 1960 at twenty-three.

YAKUZA: 1956

The Nagasu Festival, a local festival in Kumamoto prefecture, is held every year on the same date, January 15. On this date in 1956, there were many dealers with various items for sale; it was like a farmer's market with many people walking around the stalls. There was no judo practice on that date, so five of my judo friends and I attended the festival. If *yakuza* ヤクザ (members of a Japanese organized crime syndicate) walked by, people customarily moved aside to avoid them and let them pass first. If you kept on walking without moving, they would hit you with a shoulder and accuse you of hitting them and demand you apologize by giving them money. If you said you had no money, they would hit you. If you had no money and didn't want to get hit, you had to ask your friends to provide money.

This festival was held not long after the war, and society was not yet settled. The yakuza knew that my friends' and my judo dojo was near their headquarters, and they knew that my friends and I were all black belts. Most people were apprehensive around the yakuza but not my group. Three men were walking toward us, and we knew that they were yakuza because of their *haramaki* 腹巻 (belly warmer clothing), which identified them as yakuza. They also had a hat that they let rest on their head with the brim turned up all the way around. Their jackets were worn like capes without putting their arms through the armholes, and they wore *zori* ぞうり (thonged sandals) without socks.

My friend, Matsumura, was walking in the street and was intentionally hit by one of the yakuza. As black belts, we had a degree of macho, and Matsumura had intentionally not moved out of the way of the yakuza. The yakuza shouted at him. We all were interested in testing our judo skill, but while the yakuza had no strength and no guns, they did have knives. In a man-to-man fight, there is no comparison when one side has weapons, and they had long knives.

We began to argue on the street. Matsumura was the son of a fish market owner, so he headed home to get a sashimi knife. I went with him and waited outside his house while he went in to retrieve the knife. A yakuza guy had followed us to the house and was trying to see inside. When Matsumura realized the yakuza guy was outside the window, he stabbed through the storm window, which was made of wood, but thin enough that he could see and stab through it. The yakuza screamed as he fell to the ground; his intestines started coming out in a narrow string, and he grabbed them. My friend and I took the yakuza's knife from him: he couldn't move. We were angry with the guy, but we were afraid that we would be in trouble, so we removed the storm door, put him on it, and carried him to the doctor. He didn't die, and we weren't charged.

In general, the yakuza will return as a group after such an event to get revenge. I was concerned, but they did not attempt revenge. The fact that we all had black belts is the reason the yakuza did not try to get even. A black belt rank in judo was considered a serious weapon, comparable to owning a gun.

ANIMALS

Animals were a part of my life growing up both as pets and as food. My family once even kept turkeys. We started with thirty-five turkey chicks, but we discovered as they grew that male turkeys are very aggressive and will attack. When I tried to feed the turkeys, the males would run at me and peck. My mother tried to feed them, but the male turkeys attacked her, too, and when my father tried to feed them, he had the same result. We decided that the turkeys were not pets, and we would slaughter them. We offered turkeys to our friends

Three judoists. I am in the center and twenty-one years old. My cousin Chihiro Tanoue is on my left. Chihiro was with me during the yakuza fight.

and neighbors, but they were only interested in turkey meat if it had already been prepared.

My father knew how to prepare turkey, chicken, and large fish. He would call all the boys to come and watch the entire preparation process. With the turkeys, he would slit their throats leaving the heads attached and hang them upside down, drain the blood for thirty minutes, pluck them, and then skin them. My father took his shirt off because the turkeys would flap their wings as he held them, and the blood would splatter. Once the blood had all drained out, the turkeys stopped moving. When the meat was ready, we put it on the cutting board and separated it into small pieces and used the meat in soup. Neighbor cats were attracted to this meat, so my younger brother's job was to keep the cats away with a long stick. It didn't bother me to see the turkeys killed, but my mother would not let the girls watch. She told the girls that killing turkeys was boys' business.

Since there were no freezers, meat had to be eaten soon, so when a family slaughtered a pig, for example, they would share with the neighbors. We killed one turkey every two weeks, and the neighbors were delighted to get a portion of the prepared meat. Over a period of six months, we slaughtered the turkeys and distributed the meat to friends. There was no determined slaughter calendar, but neighbors would wait until some time had passed to slaughter.

We also kept two rabbits under the floor. In most Japanese houses, on the south side, there was a place to keep firewood, but we kept a certain section of that area open to make a room for two white rabbits. We used bamboo poles as bars to make a cage for the rabbits, but they dug holes and escaped. We weren't very upset when they escaped because they smelled so bad.

When I was in my late teens, I owned a German shepherd. A man I knew had a dog that had had three puppies, and he offered me one of them. The puppy I chose I named Matsu, and he grew to be a big dog. When Matsu was a puppy he cried at night, so I let him sleep with me. A basic rule of our house was that all animals could come into the house. We had a room for drying noodles, part of our business, so I put down *goza* ござ (woven rush mats) so that I could sleep with Matsu in that room. I slept there with him until he was big enough to sleep alone. We kept Matsu in back of the house so that he would not bark at the customers. My father said that a dog barking at customers was bad for business. After that, we tied him up outside beside a doghouse that my uncle had made.

I would take Matsu to a creek, and once a week I would bathe him there. At that time, I only used a brush because soap was scarce, and only people could afford to use soap. In the morning, Matsu was freed to go to the bathroom, and in the evening, he had an hour free, but I had to keep an eye on him. I was responsible for taking care of him, and I fed him miso soup, rice, and leftovers. I also gave him sweet potatoes. Often, I would pour miso soup over the rice and mix them together. There was no meat or bones for dogs then. When he barked, which he did at certain people, I had to hit him on the head. Matsu knew that he shouldn't bark. My father told me that when my dog barked at a person, not to wait to punish him: he had to be punished immediately. But I had to chase him to hit him. Occasionally I would hit Matsu too hard, and I would try to convince myself that it was educational for him, but I felt regret. My father told me that I had to hit Matsu harder, but I didn't want to, so I told Matsu, "Don't bark at those people." Matsu didn't like certain colors like red or black, otherwise he didn't bark much.

But Matsu had a dangerous habit of chasing cars. One afternoon about 3:00 p.m., I was outside, and Matsu was beside me. A three-wheeled car came by, and Matsu chased the car's right front wheel. I saw Matsu crushed by the wheel; the driver had intentionally hit him. I rushed to him, but he stood up and ran, and after searching for a long time, I couldn't find him. In the evening, my mother called me to the back door, and Matsu lay dead at the door. I cried and cried, and my father dug a grave in the back yard. I paid homage according to the Buddhist tradition: a simplified Buddhist chanting prayer. I had Matsu for only three years.

Years later and over a period of years, a client's family had three dogs die. They would buy a dog, it would die, and I would bury it. I buried all three of their dogs for them, and I told them of my experience.

Judo is useless against an aggressive dog, but I know a trick to use on an aggressive dog. Without blinking, stare at the dog with a very serious face. The dog will whimper and leave. I have done this many times with new customers' dogs. It works on all dogs: you may have to do it two or three times, but after that, they will come to be petted.

SCHOOL AFTER THE WAR

Discipline

When I was in eighth grade, the school system changed, and I was caught in the middle. In the old system, students went from grades one through eight. The new system was six years in elementary school, three in junior high, and three in high school. I felt cheated because I would have to go through three years to complete junior high rather than two. I thought, "Oh, my God!" I was among the first junior high graduates of the new 6-3-3 system.

When the war was over, we returned to our former school buildings that had been commandeered by the military, but society's values had been turned upside down, so the teachers became counselors more than academic teachers. Teachers told us that society had changed, and that we should begin preparing for a new life. In all schools, there was a place called a *hoanden* 奉安殿 (a small building that housed the Emperor's photo). Pre-war, when we students passed his picture, we were expected to stop and bow. But with the end of the war, the teachers said that there was no need to do this any longer. It was General MacArthur's custom to bow in front of the emperor's picture, however, so I continued. As I grew older, I realized that education controlled by the government can change society.

Discipline resumed after the war, as well. When I had not done my homework three times, the teacher told me to stand up, clench my teeth tightly, and put my hands behind my back; then the teacher would hit me. I had to face all the students during this punishment. I was hit three times: one cheek, the other cheek, and the first again. Some children would fall and hit their heads during this type of punishment. Some remained standing. Some cried. That was education military style: if my father were called to school to talk with the teacher, he took me home and made me sit in seiza. My father would say that I had shamed and embarrassed my family. Then he hit me on both cheeks because I had forgotten to do homework three times. That was after my teacher had already hit me. My mother's training was different: she would withhold food as punishment. She would let me eat later, but I would not be able to eat with the family at the regular hour.

Every classroom had a bamboo pole that was used as a pointer, but it commonly doubled as a paddle. Sometimes if I were disobedient at school, I would be hit with bamboo even though I didn't do really bad things. If a concept were difficult to follow, my mind drifted and the teacher would hit me with the bamboo. The teacher would yell, "KIYAMA! You're lacking concentration," and the teacher would hit me in the head with the bamboo pole. My lack of concentration often resulted in the teacher hitting me in the head. I was hit about twenty times each year during my education. At first, I would cry, but after enough times being hit, I became used to it. When I was hit in the face, the handprint would stay for a week, and classmates would say, "You got hit again!"

The girls were hit, too, but not as hard. Teachers would punish the girls by hitting their knuckles with a warning not to forget their homework or they would be in trouble again.

In sixth grade, one teacher, Mr. Fujio Nakashima, hit my best friend, Tashira, with a wooden chalk box and cut his face. Tashira tried to cover the heavily bleeding wound with his hand, but the teacher shouted, "Don't touch it!" My friend vowed he would get revenge before he graduated. His other friends asked me to assist him when he put his revenge into action because he was too small to do it alone. But by graduation day, Tashira had not gotten revenge; in fact, he thanked the teacher for having taught him, and the teacher explained why he hit Tashira. Mr. Nakashima explained that he hit him because focusing on learning is the foundation for further education.

Competition

I had a junior high classmate, Tsukuji Yoshitaka (died 2014), who was a marathon runner, and he went to the World Championship in Ethiopia in 1956. He and I were the two local track heroes, and we both aimed at the Olympic games. We competed to see who would appear in the Olympics first. Chieko, my sweetheart, saw me running with Yoshitaka all the time, and she said we looked very cool. He did not win at the World Championship because he ate something that gave him diarrhea. He had gone to Ethiopia with other university students, but they didn't have a coach with them. They took canned rice, but when they tried to find eggs to eat, they were told they would have to go to expensive places to eat eggs. He placed forty-first out of two hundred contestants. Another Japanese man placed about forty-seventh.

I broke the prefecture record in the 100-meter dash, and the record was not broken until eight years later. My younger sister, Hiroko, had made a 60-meter dash record that was not broken for twenty-one years. She also made a new record in the girls' broad jump. That record was not broken until eight years later. My oldest sister, youngest sister, and I excelled in sports. My brother, Taisei, had a remarkable running record. He carried the Olympic torch during the summer 1964 Olympics. Chieko, my sweetheart, didn't make any personal records, but she was captain when her team won, and I was captain of the boys' team when it won. Because of my athletic success, I was offered high school scholarships to Kyushu Gakuin (Christian Private High School), Arao High School, Seiseiko High School, and Kumamoto Kogyo (engineering) High School. In each case, I would have had to move away from home and live at school, and I would have had to practice sports after school.

Parts of school remained relatively consistent throughout my years there even during wartime. Once a year, during October, we had a big festival, *Undokai* 運動会 (Sports Day), and I participated from kindergarten through junior high. The students were responsible for preparing tents and chairs and drawing boundary white lines for events, and the students were required to do all the cleaning up. There were track and field events that included jumping, running, 100-, 200-, and 400- meter dashes plus various games. There was also a handicap race: a ladder was laid flat, and students had to jump through the spaces between the rungs in gunnysacks. We were divided into groups and each group had a leader who wore a leader armband. This student had to direct his group: when I was an eighth grader, I had to be a leader, but I really preferred carrying heavy things to directing people.

The prize for first place in these events was one notebook; second place, three pencils; and third place, one pencil. The prizes were always the same from first grade through junior high school. I was number one in all sports events, and I had a huge stack of notebooks because I appeared in every event and took first place in each. One year I placed first twelve times. I was a big hero from grade school through junior high school for my physical abilities. I had so many prizes that my father told me to give one to anyone who couldn't appear because of sickness or for any reason, and I felt very good about sharing my prizes. Some people never won, so I gave away many notebooks. People would see me returning home from field day proudly carrying a stack of notebooks and would ask how many notebooks I had won. I usually kept one for myself and gave one to each of my brothers and sisters. I put the notebooks on the family *Kamidana* 神棚 (miniature Shinto shrine) and clapped in the customary way and said, "Thank you" to the *kami* 神 (deities) for the support and help. I left the notebooks in front of the shrine for two or three days, and then I took them back from the kami.

Rabbit Hunting

Rabbit hunting was another school activity that occurred throughout my school years. After Undokai, we looked forward to the school's *usagigari* うさぎがり (rabbit) hunting season. Starting

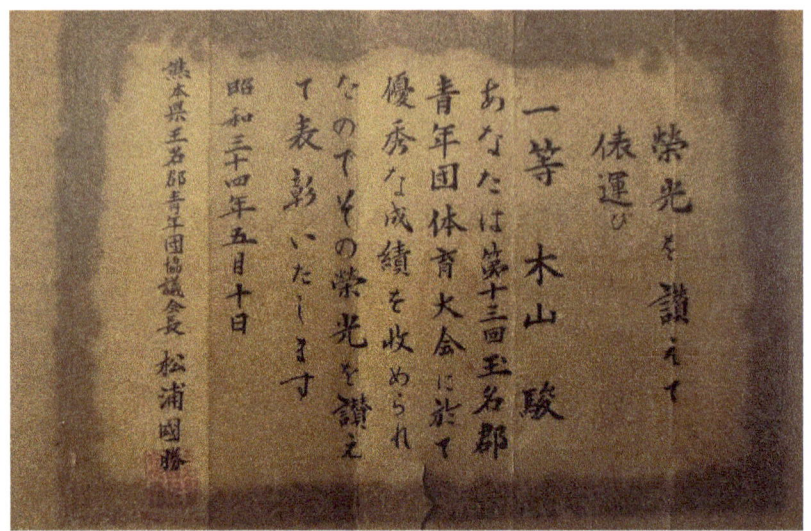

Certificate. I won this certificate for carrying and running with the most weight on my shoulder: 60 kg. of brown rice in a straw barrel.

in fourth grade, the teachers had students get up very early on a Saturday morning in November and leave with them for a two-hour walk to the mountain. Once we got to the mountain, the younger students made a semi-circle with thirty nets that were five feet tall and twenty feet long. The eighth graders made a semi-circle with their nets on the other side of the mountain from the younger students. With a whistle, the students would chant, *"choi, choi, choi"* to call the rabbits out. We continued chanting, and a few rabbits might run into the nets. If rabbits were trapped, the teachers grabbed them in the nets so that the rabbits were secure, and then we took them back to school. It wasn't necessary to kill the rabbits because they would get entangled in the nets and choke to death. We were engaged in this activity from about 2:00 a.m. until 10:00 a.m. when we left the mountain and headed back to school. Soon after we arrived, around noon, the PTA members were ready with a huge pot of rice, and we had lunch. The best day we ever had netted four rabbits. Some years there were no rabbits, so we had beef.

Dairy Work

When I was in early adolescence, I didn't have to work very much, but during the summer and winter vacations, Toshimarua Nakahara, my friend, would ask me to come and help milk his cows. Approaching his farm, the cows' droppings couldn't be smelled, but the milk smell was strong. He was the owner of the cows, and he sold the milk, but at that time, the only people who drank milk were hospitalized patients. My prefecture sent him to Denmark and later to Brazil to learn more about dairy farming.

Before we milked, we had to clean up the area and that included shoveling manure. To milk, I would sit on an apple box and use a bucket to collect the milk. First, I would wash the udder with hot water. To milk, I had to get so close to the cow that my face almost touched her, and my arms had to be relaxed and not stretched out. It took me thirty to forty minutes to milk a cow. When four people were milking, we could finish quickly, but for two, it took about five hours. By the time one cow was emptied, I would be sweating and would have to take off my jacket. On two different occasions, a fly was annoying a cow to the degree that she kicked the bucket, and I lost the entire bucket of milk. I was told that if a fly were bothering the cow, to hit the fly, because it takes two seconds for a cow to register that it is being bitten. Sometimes I would hit the fly, and it would fall into the milk. I would just fish it out and not mention that the fly had landed in the milk. When the cows defecated in the middle of being milked, the defecation splashed and hit me in the face and head. I kept my mouth shut tightly, but sometimes it went into the milk, and I fished that out. We didn't talk while we were milking the cows, but we played *enka* 演歌 (a genre of Japanese music) to calm them. The music relaxed the cows and increased the milk production. The owner liked to sing to the cows, too.

At *Obon* お盆 (a Japanese memorial festival) and New Years, Nakahara gave me an envelope containing cash of about 1000 yen. I was good at milking or any activity that required coordination.

WORKING IN THE FAMILY GRAIN PROCESSING BUSINESS

Delivery Boy

I had more regular work as a delivery boy for my father delivering bags of rice to homes. I carried the bags on a bicycle with a special back tire that was much thicker than most, but I could only carry one bag at a time. The bags with rice were various sizes and weights depending upon the size of the family having the rice refined. My delivery job started when I was in grade school, and at that time, my father lifted the heavy bags onto the bicycle, but I had to struggle to take them off by myself.

My father told me that when I delivered the bags, if the customer came out with a purse and paid me cash, to just say "thank you" and come home and keep a record of the transaction. But my father also said not to ask for payment because if the customers had the money, they would pay. I was puzzled why some people paid and some didn't. I found out later that farmers were very poor, and they had harvests twice a year: in the spring they harvested wheat, and in the fall, rice. After the harvests, many still couldn't pay in cash, so they paid with rice. Over half of the clients charged, and they would pay twice a year. So twice a year, just before Obon and New Years, I would go to the farmers' houses to collect money. At that time, farmers depended exclusively upon rice when they didn't have an income from vegetables. My father knew this and was understanding about why they might not be able to pay at the time of service. But because our refining machines used electricity, which was expensive, we needed cash to pay the electric bill, so our clients' hardships created hardship for us.

My Father's Mistake, My Future

When I was about fifteen years old, my father invested in machines that were advertised to produce a rice substitute. The company from which he was buying the machines was in Hiroshima, some distance from Nagasu-machi, my hometown. Even though food was scarce, and we needed food, I thought the machine that created the substitute rice made the product too soft. The idea was not a good one anyway because lots of food after the war came from the United States, and Japan couldn't compete. But my father seized on the idea, borrowed money, and prepared a location where all the machines would be placed. Eventually, after my father had sent the money but no machines arrived and there was no communication, he realized something had gone wrong. When he finally accepted that the machines were not coming and that he had been duped, he was deeply psychologically affected.

My Business Responsibility

About ten months after the failed business venture, when I was at school in the ninth grade, I learned that my father had had a stroke. He was considered too big and heavy, and he drank alcohol and had high blood pressure. I think the combination of losing so much money in the failed business venture and being physically unfit led to his stroke.

The amount of money my father had borrowed to purchase the equipment was equal to the amount of money in all our houses. One of the executives in the bank from where my father borrowed the money for the business respected my father, and he did some fancy footwork to save the house in which we were living. My family had been considered wealthy until my father failed in this new business. That was the beginning of the decline in my family's wealth.

My mother hid her emotions from the children. I believe she didn't want to change our lifestyle dramatically, so the menus for our meals didn't change. We always had fish even though it was expensive. She bought fish; I don't know how she did, and my father didn't say anything about her food purchases. She may have been borrowing money to get food. After his stroke, my mother took care of everything for him including bathroom needs. For six

Friends, 1950. This picture was taken during the time I was a delivery boy for my father. I am the second from the right. The second from the left was a friend whose older brother made the sheath for the knife on my waist.

months after the stroke, no one was allowed to talk with him: he was highly embarrassed.

I had been offered the high school scholarships, but after my father had had the stroke, he asked his oldest daughter's husband to tell me to give up high school because my father could no longer work as a result of the stroke, and I needed to take over his milling job. The shocking reality for me was that I had to cover for my father, and I would not be able to go to high school. My father had been milling rice to make brown rice into white, and that became my job. My younger brothers couldn't help during the day because they had to go to school, but when they had time, they did help deliver smaller loads. My father didn't discuss why I couldn't accept the scholarships with me or anyone else. The neighbors wondered, and my teachers were puzzled. My mother would respond to the question, "Why doesn't Hayawo go to high school?" with that there was a reason, but she couldn't say what.

I was no longer a student. I was a laborer.

My Work

Farmers harvested their own fields and brought their harvest to me to be milled. Usually, they brought about sixty kilos of rice in straw bags that could be milled in an hour. If the farmers had time and if I were not too backed up, they might wait for the milling to be completed. If they had a special request that needed to be done immediately, they would wait, and in that case, I would have to postpone others' work. My mother would often sit with the people who waited to keep them company.

The farmers kept brown rice at home until they needed rice to eat, and then they brought what they needed to my house for milling. They stored their rice by stacking the straw bags of rice on top of each other: the top bag was the driest and the one closest to the ground contained the most moisture. I needed to know the moisture content before I began milling the rice.

The machine took the brown rice grains and rubbed them against each other making friction and removing the chaff. The tricky part was to prevent the grains from getting broken. I tasted the grains once in a while to see if the hardness was right, and I would check that there was the correct shine on the grain. If the pressure was not strong enough, I had to send the rice through the milling process over and over to get the right gloss.

Bran was left over from the milling process, and most of it was taken by the farmers to feed to their chickens, horses, and cows. Typically, a farmhouse had a hut next to it for a cow or horse. We had quite a bit of leftover bran, and my sisters would put it into a sock with lukewarm water. Then they squeezed the bran water out of the sock to wash their face. Their faces were beautiful: of course, they were young.

We had nine milling machines, and there were two milling methods: one for the local people and one for federal rice. For the federal rice, which went to big cities, I would pour the rice into the first machine, and that machine would send the rice to other machines. For the local people, only two machines were used, and I had to run the rice through over and over again. I did lots of milling of wheat and other grains in addition to rice. The machines were running simultaneously, and I had to follow them because they broke all the time, especially the belts. I also had to oil the machines once a week. I had learned little by little when my father was healthy how to maintain and repair the machines. He didn't teach me directly, but I learned by watching. The machine area was very noisy and dirty: I had all sorts of ringing in my ears, and my face would be covered with dusty powder. Bran powder accumulated on my body, and I could scrape it off my skin. To get the bran dust out of my nose, I snorted water and then blew out lots of bran. Throughout my adulthood I have used the snorting technique to clean out my nose.

I worked seven days a week with only Obon and the first three days of January, New Year's, as vacation days. I would also take a day off if there were a family funeral. Because I was working with food, I had to move quickly, and I started milling by 7:00 a.m. My mother got up at 5:00 a.m. to prepare breakfast for me. When I got up, my breakfast was ready: miso soup, rice, and leftovers. At that time, we ate a thirty percent rice, seventy percent wheat mixture. We learned rice mixed with wheat has more nutrition. I stopped work at 5:00 p.m. so that I could get ready to go to the dojo, but if I hadn't been able to finish the day's work, I would get up an hour earlier the next day to finish. My hands had lots of calluses, and the tops of my fingers were split.

In the winter, the skin cracked on my feet because they were so dry and cold. I would heat black coal tar and press it into my feet so that cuts would be sealed stopping the air from reaching the nerves.

On special occasions when there had been a Buddhist memorial party, my mother would bring me treats from the party. Other days, she would bring me a sweet potato as a snack to eat as I worked. I had no breaks during the workday; I had to eat lunch while I worked because the machines kept running. In fact, I never took a lunch break. Even now as a gardener, I eat in the car as I go from one house to another. I am used to it.

Even though I was working alone, I was too busy to get lonely. But on school days, at 4:35 p.m., when my former classmates were returning home from high school in their uniforms, I didn't want to be seen working, because it was mortifying for me to be seen doing manual labor rather than attending school. I would hide from them in the house or behind stacks of rice. I didn't have the luxury to blame anyone, even a family member for my situation, because lenders were asking for their money back that my father had borrowed. And I did not blame my father. All I could do was to continue working, but my heart was not calm to see my classmates: I was lonely at that moment, and I felt left out. I was saddened and wondered why I couldn't be with them in high school. Much later in life, my mother told me that my father felt guilty for having me decline my scholarships to take over his work and would cry over his guilt. I was sixteen, seventeen, and eighteen years old at this time. All I could do was to keep working.

I had no expectation to be paid for my family work, and I was not paid. But when I went to a judo tournament, I would be given what money I needed. My mother said, "Eat, eat, eat. Is that enough money?" It was like a vacation. The tournament would be held in a big city where there would be lots of food. They usually took place on a Saturday or Sunday, and the other children would help in the milling because they were not in school for the entire weekend. Years later, I made a mistake with my own son who worked for me. I didn't pay him because I had never been paid, so I thought that it was natural not to pay one's child. My wife said that of course I had to pay him at least minimum wage, that it was California state law. After six months, my son wanted a raise. I learned that this is a different country with a different system.

Because I was the oldest son, at sixteen years old I was awakened to the reality of life by becoming responsible for my father's debt: I understood the difficulty of an adult's responsibilities in society. I worked at my father's mill for a total of seven years until two days before my departure for the United States at twenty-three years old.

Two

Making a Life Decision

Tradition: Atotsugi and Generosity

One day when I was still working in the family business, I could see something very emotional was occurring a few houses down. People were saying goodbye, but it was not a light-hearted goodbye: it appeared to be very serious. The economy was still so bad that there were homes people simply abandoned because they were so deeply in debt. They would often leave at night without saying a proper goodbye. But this was the middle of the day. We all knew that the family where the emotional goodbye was taking place had financial problems. When we found out that the parents were sending the daughter away to work, my brother, Futoru, gave all the cash in his pocket to her. He said, "If it is useful, just use it." The daughter would still have to work, but he gave her all the money he had in his pocket. The mother asked my brother his name, but he wouldn't tell her. He said to the daughter, "Just take the money and go."

Years later, Futoru's business (trucking) failed, and he lost everything, including the five houses my father had accumulated. After his business failed, he had a heart attack: he was sick and penniless and was forced to move into a very small one-room place. His first wife, with whom he had had three children, two boys and a girl, left him because of his business failure. His daughter had wanted to stay with him, but he said that he had nothing, so she should go with her mother. His ex-wife took the children, and she and the children stayed at her sister's house. The oldest son was soon old enough to start his own business, and his ex-wife's sister helped take care of the second son and the young girl.

Word of Futoru's failed business got around. The woman, to whom he had given money years before, heard about his business failure and tried to find him. My brother had not revealed his name, but the woman remembered my brother's yellow truck with a kanji in a circle on the truck with his name: Futuro, which means heavy or fat. After all those years, she looked very worn and was not attractive, but she was a survivor. She found my brother and said, "I want to be your helper." She said that she wanted to take care of him.

After my brother went bankrupt, he had moved to the next village, and the woman he helped all those years ago became his wife. She worked at a restaurant as a dishwasher. After his failure, my brother started a business called a *garakuta-ya* ガーベージ (junk or litter business). He would tell people to throw anything that they did not want into his place,

Futoru. Futoru is on the far right. Futoru's first wife is on the far left, and my mother is holding the baby.

Futoru's business at its peak.

Three-wheeled truck. Futoru is on the right in front of his three-wheeled truck. My family's house is to the right and behind him.

and he would repair and sell these items. He just barely made a living, but he had a $5000 Buddhist altar, a *butsudan* 仏壇, located in the only room they had. His lifestyle was very humble, but he bought the altar, so he probably had some cash just not enough to build a house.

Everyone in my family is considered generous; however, Futoru was not able to help me when I was having a hard time in the United States. Besides, during this time, Japanese believed all Americans were rich. My family assumed I was rich because the exchange rate was 360 yen to the dollar, so it was not helpful to send yen to the United States at that time. No one knew that I was having a hard time, and I am a very proud man. I chose to leave Japan; it was my idea. How could I ask for help? It was impossible.

Leaving Kumamoto

As I was working at the mill those years after my father's stroke, I was trying to determine how I would repay my father's debt. In the *Kumamoto Nichinichi Shinbun*, the local newspaper, I found an advertisement for the Tan-no Club requesting short-term agricultural workers in the United States. The ad promised that if a worker completed the three-year program, he could earn between $20,000 and $30,000. That amount of money would cover only about forty percent of my father's debt, so if I decided to go, I would have to save as much as I could of what I earned in the United States.

Almost on the spot, I made the decision to take this opportunity to help repay my father's debt. There would be farewell parties and sadness, but mind was made up.

Eight friends saw me off, and while I was very moved by their sadness at my departure, I was not focusing on them. I was looking for Chieko, my childhood sweetheart, at the entrance to the platform, and I found she was already on the train to see me off just one car away. I talked with her on the train. I wanted to ask her to wait for three years for me until I returned, but I couldn't. All I could do was shake hands, and that was the first time I had ever shaken her hand. I remember it very well. I was crying as I shook her hand. There was a popular song then, *Koogen no eki yo sayonara*, "Goodbye at the Station on the Hill."

My Japanese passport.

The lyrics of this song are about saying goodbye but with a promise of return. Many years later, during a class reunion, Chieko gave a copy of this song to me. She has an identical copy. I opened the copy of the song, and a picture of her as a schoolgirl in uniform was inside. She knew that I wanted the photo and there it was: the sailor uniform picture. Love is powerful, and this was the first time I had experienced the power of love. All these years we had no communication, but I had many dreams of her, and I hope she had many dreams of me, too.

I left Kumamoto for the United States at 4:42 p.m. on the train, and it took seventeen hours by steam train to get to Tokyo, the first leg of the journey from Kumamoto. The name of the train was Kirishima-go, and it was powered by coal.

After arriving in Tokyo, I had a chest x-ray taken at the International Red Cross Hospital in Tokyo, and then I took it to the embassy. The sealed envelope was opened at the embassy and the x-ray examined to see if I had TB or any other problem. The x-ray was clear, and I was allowed to leave the following day. Two years after I left Japan, my brother, Dairoku, tried to follow me on a work visa, but his x-ray did not pass. He had had pneumonia when he was small, and a shadow could be seen on the x-ray, so he was not allowed to leave. The concern was that if he were allowed to enter the United States, he might have developed pneumonia and not have been able to work.

I was so curious about my new life.

Three

1960–1963 August to August

Delano, California

ARRIVAL

On August 30, 1960, I flew from Hanada Airport to a small island near Alaska on a Pan American four-propeller airplane. We Japanese had been required to sign a contract that we would not change own minds and return to Japan for three years, in part, because the Japanese government had paid our way. But while the Japanese government had paid up front for the airfare, we had to pay the money back. The plane carried one hundred and thirty passengers, and the flight took nine hours. The next day, we flew to Seattle and on the same day, we flew to Fresno on a propeller plane on United Airlines. We arrived in Fresno about 1:00 p.m. and took a chartered bus with forty-five people to Delano. I was shocked to see massive vineyards lining both sides of the highway as we rode on the bus. At this moment, I felt very motivated to work hard for three years and return as much of my father's debt as I could.

One hour and a half after leaving Fresno, we arrived at Kawasaki Camp in Delano, CA. Delano is about thirty miles northeast of Bakersfield, and when I arrived there in 1960, the population was about 13,000 people. I had the impression that the area was larger than Kumamoto prefecture itself, and that America was huge. Also, the road through the vineyard was blacktop, but in Japan, it would have been a dirt road with lots of dust. By simply looking at the streets, my first impression was, "Who would dare fight against this country: the countryside is even paved!" Mile after mile, the area was paved and surrounded with vineyards. I was overwhelmed by all of this.

LIFE IN DELANO

A Japanese man owned Kawasaki Camp, and he had equipped it with dorm facilities where all the farm workers stayed. The Mexican and the Japanese dorms were close but separate, although workers from both camps ate and showered together. There were around three hundred Mexican workers, and about forty Japanese workers already working when we arrived: the Japanese had been there for about two years. The established workers wanted to show the newcomers how hot the area was, so they cracked a raw egg on the hood of a car, and the egg began to cook from the heat of the hood! All of us were impressed and maybe a little worried about the heat.

When I went to the cafeteria, I found a huge and crowded dining area. I was new, so I was not so comfortable surrounded by Mexican people. The only foreigners I had met to this point were American soldiers. In the cafeteria, eight Mexicans were cooking eggs very fast. You told them how many eggs you wanted, and they served you, but you put your own sausage on your plate. There was a mountain of bread and butter and all the milk you wanted. You ate as much as you liked, and everyone ate a huge amount: so far, so good.

But when it was time to use the toilet, I found there were forty-five commodes in a line with no privacy stalls. Japanese are not comfortable pulling their pants down in front of others. I was told before I left Japan that you could watch the guy next to you having a bowel movement. Mexicans sat comfortably on the commodes and talked with each other. There was no choice but to try to get used to it. So, I just sat quietly. The Mexicans talked to me, but I didn't know what to say. But try as I might, I became so nervous that I couldn't defecate. I pushed hard, but nothing would come out. Because most of the Japanese workers couldn't have bowel movements, they began waiting until nightfall when they would walk about a mile from the camp to defecate. We had stomachaches all day because we needed to empty our bowels. We would go into the vineyards, dig a hole, defecate, and then cover it. I trained myself to defecate at night. I would look around and then pull my pants down. After a while, people began to smell something, and the boss wanted to know what was causing the bad smell. The Japanese men kept their mouths shut.

In Delano, we slept in metal bunk beds three beds high. We were given a mattress, pillow, blanket, and top and bottom white sheets, but we were responsible for washing them on a crank and roller washing machine using soap provided in the bathroom. Because the climate is very dry, we could hang washing on wires, and it dried very fast.

I had a bottom bunk that sat on a concrete floor. The bottom bed had a box for storage, and the beds above had a bag hanging down near the sleeping person's face. There were about sixty people to one room, and there were no partitions. And to make things worse, no one was doing laundry, and the smell was horrible. The guys didn't wash their socks or clean their boots, and the entire room smelled. And as the hood cooked eggs predicted, it was very hot: huge fans helped but just a little. Thank goodness there were no mosquitos: maybe the smell was too strong for them.

I was in Delano for forty-two days, and during this time, Americans were picketing to protest cheap labor. The American farm workers were against using cheap laborers because American union workers' salaries would not go up if Japanese and Mexican workers accepted less pay and took their jobs. Our sponsors had discussions with the union workers. They did not reach an agreement, so the new recruits could not work. We had been told we would begin working immediately after our arrival, and workers were irritated because they couldn't work and didn't get paid. All we could do was eat and sleep. When we finally did start to work at $.80 per hour, we had to pay for the food we had eaten while we were idle.

Idleness led to fighting among the Mexican men. They fought in the bathroom, in the dining hall, and in the shower. There was lots of blood in the shower room from their fights. During the forty-two days I was in Delano, there were six fights. The men were young and very irritable, so they would start a fight over a tiny reason, and often there didn't appear to be any reason. There were not many outlets for the men, but there was one ... prostitutes.

VINEYARD PROSTITUTION

Every Friday evening, five or six Mexican prostitutes, *putas* in Spanish, arrived in big cars right after dinner: they did not wait for dark. A few girls would come during the week, too. The men who were interested, would leave after dinner and line up in the vineyard. Each car with a prostitute would have thirty or forty men lined up waiting, and the prostitutes would come to pick up one man, take his money, and drive him a short distance away in her car. To complete their business with privacy, the prostitutes put bath towels in the windows. *Putas* would return the first man and pick up another one. Although the new Japanese workers hesitated, the Japanese who had been there for two years got in the cars. One of the older men said to me, "I'll pay for you. My treat," but I didn't have enough nerve. Each man took ten or fifteen minutes including the round trip from the line of workers to the vineyard and back. There was never any legal trouble surrounding the vineyard prostitution. The activity was illegal, of course, but we were the bottom of the barrel, so no one cared what we did. But the women were careful. In our work area, there was one location for entering and one location for leaving. Each of these had a Mexican male guard that the prostitutes paid to watch for police. If the police were coming, the guards would wave, and the girls would scatter.

The same women came every week. The oldest two were about forty years old, and the others were in their twenties. They weren't nice looking, and no one was in good shape. I was shocked that they were not at all attractive, and the cars they came in were run down. If a woman came with a station wagon, she had done good business, and two of the women had station wagons. The remainder had large Fords, very big, long Fords with V8 engines. The men preferred the station wagons because there was more room, but as the lowest part of society, they had to accept the situation. Sometimes it got so late that some of the men would just say they would return the next time. They might have to wait three or four hours. The Mexican field workers were all under thirty, and more than ninety percent of the workers were single men. About twenty percent of the workers did not use prostitutes. If a workman were in better financial shape, he would make the thirty-minute trip to Bakersfield to hotels suited for this purpose.

RESIGNATION

At our final work destinations, the farm owners we would be working for were to take money out of our pay and send it to the Suitomo Bank who then sent it to the government to repay our flight costs. We quickly saw the reality of the situation we had been sent to and were shocked by the toilets, prostitutes, and Mexicans. Because of their behavior, we felt the Mexicans were close to animals. But we could not go home, so we accepted our situation. However horrible or shocking it appeared to us, we had signed a contract and had to abide by it. There were several men who felt extremely down. We had been given a month of orientation before we left Japan, and we had been told that the situation was bad. We were told to be ready, but we weren't.

We didn't feel tricked; however, we had gotten our hopes up that there would be something fancier because when we stopped in Alaska, everything was fancy, and the food was free. We thought that indeed this is the United States. But when we reached Delano, the story was very different. I was in shock.

Lessons on the Central Coast of California

STARTLED!

Initially I was supposed to work in Delano for three years, but the United Farm Workers Union had made that impossible. Since we workers couldn't be sent back to Japan, the plan was changed, and I was sent to the central coast of California to the farm of Mr. Masaji Eto. The

Japanese farm laborers who had arrived in Delano two years earlier, remained in Delano.

Mid-morning, October 14, 1963, nearly fifty of us left on a chartered Greyhound bus for Arroyo Grande, on the central coast of California, and we arrived there in about six hours. I was so pleased that the air was cool: such a relief from the cooking heat of Delano. Upon our arrival, various American farmers came and chose three or four men from the bus to take to their farms. When I noticed that only three of us remained, I wondered if maybe these two men were the people I would be working with.

A Japanese American woman arrived and introduced herself: Chiyo Sakamoto. I now know this woman to be Mrs. Okui. Unfortunately, she had come to pick up only one man named Kakino. Only two remained: Mr. Kurokawa and I. I was feeling lonely and at a loss as I couldn't ask the Japanese American woman questions because she didn't speak Japanese. Finally, a large Chrysler arrived with Mr. Eto driving. He talked with Mr. Kurokawa and me using a Kumamoto dialect of Japanese. I was so relieved to hear my own Kumamoto dialect. Mr. Eto told Mr. Kurokawa to get in the back and for me to ride in the front. As we were leaving Arroyo Grande, Mr. Eto used an automatic window button to lower the window: I had never seen this before.

When we reached Los Osos Valley Road leading to his home, it was pitch dark. Lights could be seen over the city of San Luis Obispo, but everywhere else was dark. After about ten minutes of driving on Los Osos Valley Road, which was lined on both sides with farmland, we made a right turn onto Eto Road. Still there was nothing to be seen.

We followed Eto Road for about one mile and finally saw a light. As we got nearer the light, I saw a building and all of a sudden, a wall of the building began to move! But it was not common sense that a wall would move. I threw my arms up and screamed loudly. Mr. Eto, startled, asked me what the matter was, and I shouted, "The wall is moving!" When Mr. Eto understood why I was startled, he laughed fully and said, "Don't worry about it." I asked Mr. Eto if the car would sleep in the house as I thought that the building was where the car slept. Mr. Eto thought my reaction was funny and later told his children. Sometime later, having never seen a garage, I realized that the garage is where the car stays, and humans go to the front door of another building.

With my suitcase in my hand, I walked toward the house: to my amazement, I recognized the house! In my village's city hall were pictures of Mr. Tamejiro Eto's farm including this house. I had just discovered that I would be working for that very Mr. Eto's son. In Japan, Mr. Tamejiro Eto, the first Eto, father to Masaji Eto under whom I would work, was well known as a man from Kumamoto Prefecture who had succeeded in the United States. In fact, there is a statue of Mr. Tamejiro Eto in Kumamoto that was unveiled with a formal ceremony, and everyone who had planned to go to the United States as a farm worker attended the ceremony. By the time we arrived in the United States, Mr. Tamejiro Eto had already died from stomach cancer, but his wife was living and was only sixty years old. My friends told me that the first Mr. Eto liked to drink with people, and he cared about other people very much. They also said that he was not satisfied with only his own success, and he was very helpful to other people. Mrs. Eto later loaned me a book written about her husband, Tamejiro Eto, and there is still a copy in the local San Luis Obispo library. At the time of my arrival in the San Luis Obispo County area, there were six cherry trees on the location of the current San Luis High School tennis courts that Mr. Tamejiro Eto had donated. They were planted at the main entrance to the high school. When the tennis courts were to be built, the trees were cut down.

That first evening at the Eto farm, Mr. Masaji Eto and his wife, Margie Eto, had prepared a welcome dinner.

Mr. Kurokawa and I went through the front door of Masaji Eto's house heading for the welcoming dinner. The first thing I saw was a black and white television set, and I was reminded that I had been told that in the United States, you can watch a movie every day. At the welcome dinner, I met Mr. Sakamoto, a single man five years older than I. He had been made a foreman by Mr. Eto and had been working for him for six years when I arrived. He was a distant relative of Mr. Eto's, and he was from Eta-mura village, Tamana-gun (county). In the car, Mr. Eto had told us that we would be served tuna sashimi. What a welcome sight: the sashimi filled a huge platter, and it was made all the more special because this was the first time Mr. Kurokawa and I had eaten Japanese rice and other Japanese food for forty-two days. I ate until I was satiated.

Mrs. Eto said for us to just eat sashimi and relax. I was quite amazed and delighted that I could eat sashimi because at that time in Japan it was too expensive. People would only be able to afford sashimi for weddings or some other special event. My hope for a fancier life was renewed.

The only guests at the dinner were Mr. Sakamoto, Mr. Kurokawa, and I. I asked Mr. Sakamoto to confirm that this was the house of the famous Tamejiro Eto, and he confirmed it. Mr. Tamejiro Eto was recognized as *kami-sama* 神様 (deity). As soon as I discovered that I was at the home of the famous Mr. Tamejiro, I felt positively committed to work hard. Dinner lasted about two hours, and then Mr. Sakamoto suggested that we leave and walk to camp. On our way to the camp, Mr. Sakamoto told Kurokawa and me that there were two people from Nagasaki Prefecture living in the building we would be living in who had been there fourteen months.

MR. AND MRS. ETO: FIRST GENERATION

Mrs. Take Eto, wife of deceased Tamejiro Eto and mother to Masaji, told me the following story. Mr. Tamejiro Eto was born in Chida-mura, the county of Kamoto-gun, and the prefecture Kumamoto-ken. In 1902, Mr. Eto came to the United States alone, but back home, his family thought it was time for him to get married. Mr. Eto sent his picture, and the photo was passed around to all the eligible young ladies. One young woman, Take, expressed interest. During their generation, love marriages were almost unknown, and there were always *nakkodo* 仲人 (matchmakers) around to help people find spouses. Before she made her decision, she and her family checked Mr. Eto's relatives and family to see if there were any psychological or medical problems and found him to be a suitable match. She asked her parents what they thought about this young man, and they felt his family was acceptable; therefore, he would be a reasonable man to marry. With her parents' agreement, she trusted everything would be all right and volunteered to go to the United States and marry him.

At age eighteen, she left Yokohama for San Francisco, and it took her thirty-one days of travel by boat. On the long trip, she was wondering what kind of man her future husband was. When she arrived in San Francisco, Mr. Eto met her and offered his hand to shake; she thought she was shaking hands with a rock because his calluses were so thick. She was completely shocked because she realized that meant that he was working hard like a dog. She was so overwhelmed that she couldn't look at his face. The old car in which he drove her from San Francisco to Los Osos, her new home, was another hint about how difficult her life would be.

When she arrived in Los Osos, she didn't find a house but rather a straw hut. There were six horses housed in half of the hut, and she and Mr. Eto slept in the other half. There was no electricity in their home, and it was pitch dark in Los Osos at that time. She said she had thought that Japanese farmers were poor, but they at least had electricity. Every night, she would face Japan and look at the sunset and cry because she knew she could never go back. There was nothing in Los Osos. The owls sang in the night, and she would cry as they cried their eerie song; in fact, she said she cried for two years straight. Every day was an incredible amount of work. At that time, love was not important; it was a luxury. They thought it was fate for them to be together, and they were thankful for each other.

Mrs. Eto went on to tell me a story involving her bathing and farm workers. Filipinos could come to the United States to work as farm laborers at that time, and Mr. Eto hired them. The Filipino men could not bring wives with them, however, so they probably longed for women. When Mrs. Eto got into the bath, an old oil barrel, she realized that the Filipino workers were peeking. She asked Mr. Eto for help, and he tried, but he was unsuccessful. She was not afraid of anything, however, so she decided to fight by throwing water on them as they peeked. That, too, was a failure because she had to stand up to throw the water exposing her breasts. She said they were even more encouraged! She just gave up after a while as the Filipinos would peek every day, regardless of what she or Mr. Eto did or said.

Mrs. Eto said that when she and Mr. Eto got older, they were invited to Japan by the government because of all the help they had given Japanese people in the United States. Mr. Eto was given the *kun-yonto* 勲四等 (Emperor's recognition). He donated money to his village, Chida, in Kumamoto-ken, after his success in the United States. He also built a building for the Chamber of Commerce and created a society called *Gojokai* 互助会 (benefit society) for the purpose of helping each other. There is a bust larger than human size of him in his village.

DOMESTIC LIFE IN CAMP

Mr. Sakamoto knocked on the door of the building in which Kurokawa and I would be staying. We went in, and we greeted each other in the American way even though we were all Japanese: we shook hands. We learned that an extra bed belonged to Sukeo Oosawa, a student from California Polytechnic State University, the university in San Luis Obispo. Oosawa was not there the night that Kurokawa and I arrived, and the two men from Nagasaki told Kurokawa and me to simply ignore Oosawa. They said he was stuck up because he was a college boy, and he felt free to give advice. When we finally did meet him, he told us that America is a tough place and to be ready for it. I never learned to like Oosawa because he always made it clear he was a student and therefore superior to the rest of us. In addition to that, he had a '57 Chevrolet, and when we needed to do laundry, shopping, or any other activity that required a car, Oosawa first asked for gas money. There were two Chinese restaurants in San Luis Obispo, but we most often went to the one called Mei Hung Low. If Oosawa took us in his car, we had to buy his gas and dinner. Another reason we had to buy his dinner and gas was that he was the only one who could speak English, and he had to interpret for us. Oosawa worked weekends when he had no exams. Because we had to buy gas for Oosawa, I became aware that gasoline was twenty-three cents a gallon. And because I bought milk, I knew it was twenty-three cents a gallon: the same price! In my memory, milk and gasoline were always the same price. Oosawa later returned to Japan and found a job at the Yamaha Corporation. His work involved an engine to pump water from a lower to a higher place.

The Nagasaki men offered coffee or tea, and I requested tea. Mr. Sakamoto told me that I needed to get up early the next morning after the welcome dinner, and I was told that the job in the morning would be to connect the pipes of a sprinkler system.

Mrs. Eto had taught the two men from Nagasaki how to cook rice on the stove, and these two taught the remainder of us. The first evening meal I had at the camp with the other workers was a sukiyaki type meal: beef mixed with soy sauce and sugar. There was a huge refrigerator, and for the first week or so, the Nagasaki men cooked while Mr. Kurokawa and I washed the dishes. Later, we took turns cooking, but since I didn't know how to cook, Kurokawa helped me. When it was my turn, I always had to have help. I had plenty to eat at this time of my life. In Japan, my work had been inside, and even though the work on the farm was much harder, I was always happy to be outside and always ate a grand amount.

Beef, beef, beef: I liked it very much. We put it in a frying pan with garlic, salt, and soy sauce. Once a month, Mrs. Eto went shopping for herself and for us at the Nishi market, also called the West Market, in San Luis Obispo, which was a Japanese market. We were able to get basic Japanese foods like soy sauce, miso, rice, pickled daikon, rice, and Azuki *Zen-zai* 小豆 善哉 (dessert soup). We fixed many eggs for breakfast and a big bowl of hot rice.

We got up early from April through October, by 3:30 or 4:00, to start work before sunrise and had no time to cook. So, the night before, the *senpai* 先輩 (senior) prepared miso soup for the following morning. Even that early in the morning, I ate a big breakfast. Since there was no automatic rice cooker, the rice had to be cooked the previous day. There was a thick kettle about ten inches deep with a heavy glass lid in which to cook the rice. We had six burners on the stove, and to start the fire, we turned the gas on and struck a match. To cook the rice, we made a strong fire under the water first, put the rice in the boiling water, and when the water cooked down to be level with the rice, we made the fire weak. The lid was put ajar, and when the water was all gone, we put the lid back on and turned the heat off. We would wait ten minutes before eating the rice. In the morning, we heated the meat and vegetables that the men had prepared the night before, but the rice was cold. I have always believed that eggs are good for building energy, so I added two eggs to my meat and vegetables every day. Having two eggs per day is a habit I continue today.

In Japan, we could only eat meat on a few special occasions a year, and that meat would be in soup, but at the Eto farm, we could daily eat a huge chunk of meat. I was very satisfied, and I felt lots of power and energy. I was eager to work because I had a clear goal to pay my father's debt, and I could eat as much as I wanted: fruit, milk, and meat. At that time, I was never negative about my situation. During the war, eating had been my main concern, and now, again, eating was my number one concern. After the war and before I left Japan there was a shortage of protein. I would eat miso soup with pickled daikon and rice with wheat in it. I was not hungry because I was full with either *hakumai* 白米 (white rice) or *mugi-meshi* 麦飯 (rice with wheat) but not with protein. An egg was a precious food. When I went to a judo tournament, however, my mother prepared a three-egg *tamago-yaki* 玉子焼き (egg cooked and rolled).

I still remember the taste of the beef at the camp. I asked the other men, "Do you eat this every day?" They said they did, and I was very encouraged and looked forward to dinner each day. Kurokawa and I washed dishes so that the senpai could prepare breakfast for the next day. We often cooked pork in miso soup for the next day's breakfast, and we did not refrigerate it. Whoever got up first heated the soup. Rice had been cooked the night before. When we got up, we cooked six eggs in the miso soup. If there were no eggs cooked in the soup, I would eat a raw egg in the cold rice. I drank green tea for breakfast, but the others drank soda. I didn't have soda until later in day.

LABORING ON THE FARM

Learning the Ropes

The harvest was almost over when I arrived at the Eto farm, so I was able to get up at 7:00 a.m., quite a bit later than during harvest time, and begin more gradually. When a new group arrived as harvesting began, those men had a harder time.

In the morning before work, we had to move our bowels, but we only had three minutes to complete the job because we had only one toilet. At least it had a door, which made the job possible. At the camp, the oldest person was expected to go to the bathroom first, but if it were an emergency, anyone, regardless of age, was allowed to go. I had been warned to eat plenty of vegetables because I would be eating lots of meat and could become constipated. Constipation could mean a bowel movement in the middle of the day. By law, we did have a portable bathroom on the farm, but no one liked it if a worker were gone long. The senpai told me that if I noticed a hint of constipation to drink two glasses of orange juice at night, and a bowel movement was guaranteed the next morning.

My first morning, as I had been told, my job was to connect the water pipes of the irrigation system to water the sugar beets. After only one hour of connecting and disconnecting the irrigation pipes, my skin started splitting and bleeding. I had no gloves the first day. The senpai wanted me to work the first day with no gloves to convince me that I needed them, and so I would not forget them. He told me gloves would keep the dirt and sandy soil out of my open skin.

Even though we didn't work directly under the spray of the sprinkler system, we had to wear raincoats and boots to avoid getting soaked while connecting the 20-foot-long six-inch water pipes. There were sixteen rows of sprinkler, and I unhooked them and moved them to another sixteen rows that had not been watered the previous night. Moving the sprinklers took nearly three hours. After redistributing the pipes, we began weeding sugar beets. My hands were already bloody and blistered, but I weeded until lunchtime. That first day, we had a one-hour lunch break and even though my hands were sore, I didn't feel tired at all. I ate twice as much as the others, and I was very proud that I didn't feel tired.

Lunch was at 12:00 every day. In general, the length of lunchtime was determined by the price of vegetables: when prices were high, we would have a shorter lunch break because we had to harvest more and faster. We always ate at the farm, and when lunch was short, Mrs. Eto prepared sandwiches.

For ten days, everything felt so new and was a learning process. The Mexicans worked so fast, and I felt pressure to go fast, but I could not remove all the weeds. It took me about one year to be able to keep up the Mexican workers. The senpai's speed was the same as the Mexicans. I felt that since we were all being paid the same, I needed to do as well as the Mexicans. We weeded until it was too dark to see.

I had a difficult time sleeping during my first few nights because I was excited, but the senpai went to sleep quickly, so I had to be quiet in the dark. Those first nights I was restating to myself that my reason for being there was to return my father's debt. I continued to remind myself not to forget why I had come to the United States.

As time passed, we settled into a routine: the *senpai* went to bed at 9:00 or 10:00 p.m. while the rest of us went to bed at 11:00 p.m. I was not homesick during this time because I knew I was not permitted to go back to Japan, so I just didn't think about being homesick. I considered my life on the farm a test whether I could survive this life or not.

Since Mr. Eto was the overseer as well as owner, he directed all the workers and was up earlier than anyone. He watched. And his foreman, carefully chosen Mr. Sakamoto, would not permit a sloppy job. Mr. Eto was also a clever businessman. The price of lettuce fluctuated, and he knew that some days lettuce would be a big hit, so rather than harvesting it all at once, he did a little at a time. Since we were working so early, the dew was still present, and the iceberg and romaine lettuces were fresher and brought a better price. Every day we harvested five hundred boxes with each containing two-dozen heads. When harvesting was completed, my job was to use the Caterpillar to till the soil to compost stalks and roots left after harvest. We would soon plant in the same spot after vegetables were harvested. Mr. Eto observed what other farmers were doing, too. Typically, rain could stop farm workers from working, but Mr. Eto sometimes asked us to work when it rained because other farmers did not have their men work, and the limited supply caused the price of Mr. Eto's produce to go up. If we didn't work, we weren't paid.

Camp

The Japanese and Mexican camps were located very close to each other, but the Japanese camp was in much better shape. We didn't have much in the way of furniture, but we did have a long table and benches to sit on. Six people could sit on each side, and it was on that table that I could write letters. The student had his own desk. Others built their own bookshelves and put their books there. Behind the Japanese workers' backs, the Mexicans were complaining about their housing situation. But the Japanese didn't wear shoes inside, so it was cleaner, and it was neater as they organized their clothes and shoes. The Mexican's place was a huge mess because they worked seven days a week and did not clean. I think there was a class difference between the Japanese and Mexicans, but I liked their heart.

After I started to understand Spanish, the Mexican workers told me their homes in Mexico were worse than their living conditions on Eto's farm. We were all paid the same: $.80 per hour. If they worked on the Eto farm for three months, they didn't have to work for the rest of the year to support six family members in Mexico. There was a huge gap in what they could earn in Mexico compared with the United States.

After work, Mr. Sakamoto, the foreman and higher ranked than the *senpai*, usually gave us Japanese workers and the Mexicans a ride in the pickup to our camp. I could feel sweat and salt on my face and back. The Mexicans didn't take a shower after work because they were so tired that they went to sleep with their shoes on. They smelled bad after perspiring all day: the body can smell very strong! Riding inside an enclosed truck, I could smell one of the other guys, a Mexican, so I told him to take a shower, but he didn't do it. The Mexicans had a shower available, but showering wasn't their custom. The Mexican and Filipinos had a shine of wet oil on their bodies rather than salt. For me, they had a rotten garlic smell. The two groups smelled different, but they both smelled bad. The Filipinos probably smelled worse. Often, when they worked ahead of me, the wind would carry their smell. All day I felt nauseated, so I worked faster and was able to get ahead and avoid the smell. I could detect no smell from the Japanese: I think food and whatever else is taken into the body determines body smell. The Mexicans liked to drink Tequila every night, and they smoked. Only one Japanese man out of six smoked. I think the things put into the body contribute to body smell.

We Japanese showered every day. Usually the two *senpai* showered first, then I showered followed by the younger men. We had a shower in the one bathroom shared by six people; by the fourth person, the water started getting cold. Oosawa, the student, usually came home late, but if he were there when we were ready to shower, he would be the first to take a shower. While he arrived at the Eto farm first, he was younger than the *senpai*, and by custom, he should have waited.

We would ask, really hire, Oosawa to take us shopping for necessities one day a week when the stores were open until 9:00 p.m. Sometimes, we would make a shopping list, and he would buy our items on his way back from school, and then we let him eat the food we had prepared. The other men asked Oosawa to take them to the laundry in San Luis Obispo to do their washing, but I did my own by scrubbing the clothes and letting them dry in the sun.

After our showers, we talked about cooking. We had different tastes so Mr. Kurokawa and I, who had similar tastes, cooked together. The two *senpais* cooked their own meal, but we shared rice. The student usually ate sandwiches he bought outside the camp; however, he always checked our pot first, and if he liked what he saw, he asked to eat. We let him just to keep the peace. We put up with him because we all had a weakness in our limited English language skills and because we had to rely on him for transportation. Sometimes Oosawa didn't clean his own dishes, and we left his dishes unwashed. He would say, "While you wash yours, why don't you wash mine?" He was big headed and cocky.

Pressure

The senpai and the other Japanese workers went to Oceano to find Mexican prostitutes who were available at bargain prices; the Oceano women charged $5.00. I was tempted a little bit, but the purpose of my being in the United States and the thought of my mother begging the lenders for extra days to return money, prevented me from going. I could hear my mother telling the men that she only had 20,000 yen to buy her children shoes and shirts. I had a sexual appetite greater than the average man. So deep in my heart, I wanted to go, but my mother's voice came to me. After two years of my being there, even the newer guys went, and I was left alone. They said, "If you are a man, this is the typical thing to do." I resisted their pressure. I told them that I had a specific goal and couldn't spend the money, but I didn't tell them the reason or what the goal was. As a Japanese man, I was expected to act as a member of the group, and the other men didn't like my independent behavior.

But six months before the senpai left, I told the men the real reason I wouldn't act as part of the group: I explained my family situation. I explained that even though I had wanted to join the men, I couldn't. Everyone had come to save money. We all came with a clear goal to save money because in Japan, the oldest son would inherit everything, and none of them was the eldest. They cried when I told them why I had not joined them. One man said that he had come with the same goal, but money accumulated and since no one was watching him, he decided to play a little bit. At first, he had been going straight, but eventually he went to Oceano. They apologized and said that I didn't need to go with them. They had been travelling to Oceano once a week or once every two weeks for this purpose, but some of the men decided to quit going because of my determination.

There were about eighty Japanese farm workers in San Luis Obispo County. Only the student got *rin-byō* 淋病 (gonorrhea). While it was not easy to stick to my goal, I was strong and am glad that I didn't use the prostitutes. My father believed that his son would not behave in that way: in fact, my father would have literally killed me for such behavior. My father's principle was that if you touch a woman, you marry her. But my father's severity was not as powerful as the tenderness of my mother. It was my mother's voice that stopped me.

The Work Environment

In the winter in Los Osos we grew broccoli, cauliflower, and sugar beets because they are frost resistant. The winter vegetables were harvested in February and March. In March we planted most of the summer vegetables, but lettuce work began late April and lasted until October. The farmers knew how many people were needed for working, so they would stagger planting so that the hired help would be enough to manage. When the lettuce plants were between seven and eight inches high, we would thin them. I was required to use a short-handled hoe for three years. Because there had been so many back problems from the short-handled hoe used in thinning, a law was passed in 1965 outlawing it, but before the passage of the law, we used it.

To thin plants, the short-handled hoe required bending over at the waist and bending the knees. The short rows took two hours to make a round trip, and the long rows, four hours, but even one hour caused back pain. After finishing a row, I would lie down. I had prepared mentally for this work but not for all the physical demands. The Mexicans would simply stand up and look around for about three minutes and go back to work. I thought that it must be painful for the Mexicans, too, but maybe they had become used to it. Even though they didn't keep themselves clean and they smelled bad, after experiencing the pain in my back, I decided to respect the Mexicans because in this job, they were better than I was. The short-handled hoe was fast, but I had excruciating back pain for the entire three years I used it. I would lie down in the mud to stretch my back. We Japanese all did. I would look at the blue sky and lie there for three to five minutes. I wrapped cotton material tightly around my waist for support and warmth. We didn't take any oral pain medication, and we all had pain. When the morning work was over, we would go to lunch, but I had to straighten up very slowly as did all the beginners. After the full day's work was over, I kept my body warm, and the pain left. I was young, in my early twenties, and the pain did not linger into the night. Other people put a medicated pad on their back. I think because of my judo training, I was spared too much discomfort. I had learned at a young age that my body can take more than I think. At Eto's farm, I ate beef, eggs, meat, and milk: if I had been eating a traditional Japanese diet, my body would not have lasted. In comparison, my job today as a gardener is easy.

In the hour we had for lunch, we ate leftovers from the previous day: ham, turkey, or maybe miso soup and milk. We didn't have time for talking or for taking a nap, so we ate, washed the dishes, and went back to work. I didn't want to wash dishes, so I put everything on one dish. We were supposed to rotate dish washing, but it always led to arguing, so we ended up doing our own dishes. After our evening meal, we talked for about one hour and got to know each other.

We had had to sign an agreement at the American embassy in Japan that we would not fight, a general requirement. But one night, there was a fight: a guy from Nagasaki and one from Kumamoto fought over dirty dishes. Everyone was dead tired, and the Kumamoto guy said that he would do his dishes the next day, but the Nagasaki guy said that he must do them that evening. The Kumamoto guy got a bloody nose, and his face turned totally black. The next day we lied to Mr. Eto about the physical signs of the struggle.

After I had been on the job for one year, Mr. Eto changed his paying method: he began to pay according to how many rows we had completed. The Mexicans began working at 3:00 a.m. When I started at 5:00 a.m., I was about one hundred feet behind the Mexicans.

MR. ETO, THE MAN

Mr. Eto knew the situation in Japan: if there were more than one son, then the oldest son would inherit the family's wealth and responsibilities, and the other sons would get a much smaller portion of the inheritance and be in a very weak position. So, his view was that he was helping those second and thirds sons. If they were hired in the United States, Mr. Eto knew that the dollar to yen exchange was good for the workers, and they could make money quickly. After three years, they could have enough to build a house in Japan. I don't know if it were kindness or not, but Mr. Eto knew the job he gave the younger siblings would help the men. As a human being, I did not have much respect for the second Mr. Eto: he was a calculating man. All the Mexicans were illegal, and Mr. Eto knew it, but it was cheaper to hire them. He donated to the Buddhist community, but he was not generous if he knew that there was no payback for his generosity. He was not a sincere Buddhist, but because of his money, he was a big shot in the church.

On Thanksgiving and New Years, Mr. Eto invited all the Japanese workers and their families to dinner. We would work until two hours before dinner, go home, shower, and change our clothes. Thirty or forty people would be there for dinner, but he did not invite the Mexican workers. I felt that the Mexicans should have been invited, too. I had heard about racial prejudice in the US, but I thought it was only against Blacks. I found it was against Mexicans, too. I asked the meaning of Thanksgiving: I found that it was a celebration giving thanks for the harvest. When I realized the Mexicans were excluded, I couldn't enjoy dinner very much. Mr. Eto's father, the first Mr. Eto, was a very different man.

DRIVER'S LICENSE

The greatest number of people who came at one time using the Tan-no Club that I had used, was twelve hundred men. Most of the Japanese men who came to work had a farming background. In my case, my mother's older brother was an agricultural co-op head, and he had arranged the paperwork for me to go to the United States to work. Men were sent to various states and were called

Tanki Nogyo Romusha. Mr. Eto required that we sign a contract that we would not get a driver's license or drive a car for three years, as did the Japanese government. Mr. Eto was sponsoring us, and if there had been an accident, he would have been liable. Also, we were uninsured, and if we had a car accident, the entire program would fail. On the other hand, if you had a license and drove a produce truck, you were paid twice as much per hour.

Despite his own contract, Mr. Eto and all the other farm owners, gave workers an opportunity to get a license so that the farm owners would not have to hire a more expensive American driver. If American men were hired, Mr. Eto had to pay over-time, so he ultimately changed his mind and allowed us to get a driver's license.

Mr. Eto wanted me to get my license so that I could drive produce to Oceano about twenty minutes away from his farm. I had taken the written driving test three times and failed each time: it was in English, and I couldn't read or write English. Mr. Eto said to keep trying and that he would pay for the test for a fourth attempt. The fourth time I took it, I had memorized the answers, but the problem was that on each exam the questions were in a different order. I had memorized the first word and the last word of the answers and was able to pass it the fourth time. All of us workers struggled to pass the test, and we all settled on this method of memorization. I had finally gotten my license, but I am still concerned about taking the test which I must as I age. My only hope is to take the test in Los Angeles where the test is offered in Japanese.

WHILE I WORKED: THE NEWS, LOCAL AND WORLD

When I was at the Eto farm we sometimes listened to the news on television at lunchtime as we ate: Oosawa would interpret. On October 29, 1960, the Cal Poly football team was in an airplane crash. I had watched the Cal Poly football team play two or three times; the crash was a huge story. A funeral service was going to be held on campus, and I wanted to attend this service. Since I couldn't understand English and needed an interpreter, I went to the campus service with Oosawa.

In 1962, another news story that I heard was that Kenichi Horie had crossed the Pacific Ocean by boat in ninety-four days, the first person ever to do this alone. But he had done it without a proper visa. For a Japanese person, the seriousness of the lack of proper visa was of more importance than the successful solo sail. The Japanese Consulate said it was an embarrassment that Horie had crossed without a visa, but the citizens of San Francisco welcomed him. I think because of that, he was given a visa. He later crossed the Atlantic and Indian Oceans, and he sailed around the world.

On November 22, 1963, during a lunch break, I saw live on television the assassination of John F. Kennedy. I was shocked to see such an event on television.

ILLEGAL AND ILLEGALS

There were fifteen to twenty illegal Mexicans on Mr. Eto's farm; during the early winter, they went back to Mexico and returned in February. Essentially, white Americans didn't do farm labor. If they did any work on the farm, they were tractor drivers. During work, the Mexican workers were very unmotivated unless the foreman was there; they would just talk to each other. In fact, they were devoted to not working without a foreman present. Without exception, they didn't work if there were no overseer: they were not interested in working at all. Maybe it is a national characteristic; I noticed they are very play oriented. Most of the Mexicans working on the farms only had three years of elementary school education, so they had no other work options available to them. They said that their Spanish was not good Spanish meaning it was not proper Spanish. I came to be able to communicate with their Spanish, but it was not useful outside the camp.

To make lots of money, Mr. Eto did illegal things; primarily, he hired lots of illegal Mexican workers, and when the border patrol came, the Mexicans hid between the rows of celery. If the border patrol officer saw someone running, he fired a shot into the air, which stopped the man dead in his tracks. The border patrol officer then handcuffed him, and the captured man would be sent back to Mexico. The border patrol was only equipped to transport twenty illegals, so when they had more than that, they had to call for a van. At Eto's, there were only between fifteen to twenty illegals, but when certain vegetables were ready to be harvested, more illegal Mexicans would come from Oceano to help. In Santa Maria, the border patrol caught between fifty and eighty people every time they checked. The border patrol would take the illegal Mexicans to San Diego and drop them off, but they returned after three days and were back at work. The border is fenced and almost one mile wide, so I asked the old timers how they could get back. I was told they would swim in the ocean. There was also a business run by Mexican Americans that helped them, and from Los Angeles they used a train or bus.

Once when we were harvesting broccoli, Mr. Eto began waving vigorously. That was the signal that the immigration people were coming. On this day, the Mexicans began escaping into the woods and ditches where they remained very quiet. Only the Japanese continued to work at this point. The border patrol officer shot his gun twice into the air and shouted something in Spanish. The well-experienced Mexicans didn't come out, but several of the newer Mexican workers were caught, handcuffed, and taken away. After the officer had left, we Japanese shouted "All clear," and the remaining Mexican workers came out.

In 1965, the government began to punish employers of illegals. When that began, Mr. Eto hired white men to guard the entrance of his farm about one mile from where the work was going on. With a walkie-talkie, the white employee would let Mr. Eto know that the border patrol was coming. He would have the Mexicans hide, and when the Border Patrol looked with binoculars, they saw only Japanese men.

For the first year, I did not pass judgment on people or groups of people. But by the second year, I was convinced that the Mexicans were unmotivated and lazy: their level of interest in work was so different from the Japanese workers. While their hearts were good and they were very nice men, they had no self-dignity and lacked a sense of responsibility: no foreman, no work. Mr. Eto recognized the fact and accepted it. They know how to work hard, but once they reached a certain speed, they didn't improve; the Japanese workers kept trying to improve. It took me ten months to a year to reach the speed the Mexican laborers were working. All the Japanese farm workers worked hard, but they did not intend to do that type of work for all of their lives. Mr. Eto told me that if he hired Mexicans, they would work for him their entire lives, but Japanese planned their future, and they would leave. It was not a matter of liking or disliking Japanese or Mexicans: Mr. Eto knew and accepted the reality.

I don't have any Mexican friends from my working years; most of the men were older than I was. Near the end of my time at the Eto farm, the new men coming were younger than those who were there when I started. By now, the workers who were there when I arrived have died. There was an illegal Mexican named Chavez who had been coming for more than twenty-five years. After leaving the farm, I met him once during the 1970s after I had begun my own gardening business. I went to the Eto farm to see him. I have heard since that he has died.

CHEATING MEXICANS

Sometimes on the weekend the Mexicans would invite the Japanese workers for tortillas: the preparation was dirty, but the tortillas were delicious. They cooked over an open fire. I liked the food they fixed, but it was very spicy. They used hot sauce on the chicken, and I would ask for the mild sauce. During the weekend, the Mexican men talked about their families. Before March, during rainy days when we couldn't work, we would get together with the Mexicans, and sometimes we Japanese would invite them to our place. The Mexicans always commented on how clean our place was kept.

When the Mexicans came to our place, everyone played poker. We kept wondering why jokers always seemed to go to the Mexicans' hands, but after a year, we found that they were cheating. We caught the moment one of the men was cheating, and I said, "You have the joker: show it!" In the end, I used *hadaka-jime* 裸絞 (naked strangle), a judo technique to choke the man who was cheating. I didn't go so far as to cause him to pass out, but I stopped *just* before he passed out. I let go, and then I choked him again.

The guy was nearly lifeless, so I sat on the floor behind his back, and I put my arms under his armpits, pressed my knee against the fourth and fifth vertebrae and with force pulled him in toward me. He gasped and began breathing again. The three other Mexicans looked at each other, and I told them to give him a glass of water. They were so shocked that they couldn't speak. The Mexican had gained eight dollars using his dirty trick. The others counted eight dollars out and gave it to me. Even this didn't end their cheating, but after that, our relationship with the Mexicans got better because I had showed strength.

ACCIDENT AND REHAB

Once during the winter broccoli harvesting time, when the ground was muddy, a tractor got stuck in deep mud. I was trying to dislodge the tractor, but my leg was unstable, and I twisted my knee. I think my judo training may have weakened my knee. With a swollen and extremely painful knee, I went to French Hospital in San Luis Obispo, and I was told I had to have an operation. When the doctor, Dr. Keith, opened my knee up, he found the ligament was destroyed. I stayed in the hospital for five days and had a month of rehab. I only had workmen's compensation during that time which was about half my regular pay. It was enough to eat, but it was not enough to send any money home.

When I was staying in the camp recuperating, the Tenri-kyo Buddhist monk came and gave a Buddhist prayer, chanting and touching my knee. The priest looked so serious and said that in two or three days everything would be healed, but it did not help at all in the end. I was stuck in the farm workers' living quarters during my recovery time. The doctor told me to begin walking when the pain was gone, so even during the rainy time, I was walking. I had cabin fever and was worried about my father's debt. We had a small black and white TV in our quarters, but it only got English-speaking channels. I watched the *Ed Sullivan Show*. I couldn't understand anything, but I could see what they were doing. (Many years later I went to a show in Laughlin, Nevada, where a guy was pretending to be Ed Sullivan. While I was there, I gambled, the only time in my life.)

Near the end of my rehab, Mr. Eto got permission from the county to kill deer off season because they were eating his lettuce, and he gave me a job to do. The deer would come near dawn and then again near sunset. They liked to eat Romaine lettuce, and they ate only the good part of the lettuce. As my knee was nearly healed but I couldn't yet do farm labor, Mr. Eto told me to go to the farm and shoot the deer. He told me to aim at the heart and shoot. I shot seven deer, and each time the Mexicans dashed into the field and cut the deer's necks to drain the blood. They prepared the meat very quickly and took it all. They carried the meat in a plastic bag, and one man would dig a hole and bury the waste. They cooked the deer meat, but it smelled bad, so I couldn't eat it. I didn't like to kill deer because they are so cute. During the winter, Canada geese came, and Mr. Eto, his son, and I went out to shoot geese. I enjoyed that.

COMMUNICATION WITH HOME

In 1963, a cable was laid to connect Japan to the US through Los Osos, but I made no phone calls home until I asked the Eto's to use their phone in 1965. I got my first phone in 1968. I only had time to write a few letters, but my mother wrote many times, and my sisters wrote. I wrote to my younger sister once a year, and two months before I returned to Japan, I wrote asking whether Chieko had married. When my sister wrote back and said she had, my brain was emptied. When I left for the US, my former girlfriend's brother had seen me off at the border between Kyshu and Honshu. Chieko was not married at that time. Her brother wanted to know my plan, so he had seen me off so that we could talk about it. He wanted to know if I could promise to marry Chieko, and I said that I couldn't promise. It was a difficult time in Japan. She had been made a proposition by the head of the JR train station in Kumamoto. If she were to marry him, then her younger brother would get a job. After two years and three months, my younger sister, Hiroko, who was friends with Chieko, told me that Chieko was very sad about her marriage. I cannot confirm what she said, but my sister said Chieko was crying and that she had been pressured to marry. She could not be an obedient daughter and disappoint her father by denying a job for her younger brother. After that, I decided I would live in the United States. While working, I could forget that she had gotten married, but when work was over, I cried in bed. I thought that after a few months the sadness would ease, but it didn't. I continued to suffer.

Four

First Work Tour Concludes

Planning to Return

My pay at the Eto farm increased during my first years there but very little. The first year and ten months I worked for Mr. Eto, I was paid $.80 per hour. The last fourteen months I was paid $1.25 per hour. During harvest time, the hourly system was changed, and I was paid per box. From April through October, this change increased my salary to about $6.00 an hour. I worked eighteen hours a day, seven days a week. I had asked for extra work and was asked to drive a Caterpillar late at night and into the very early morning tilling the soil. I got up at 5:00 a.m. and was usually sleeping only four or five hours a night. At harvest time, everyone worked a minimum of ten-hour days.

My three years were nearly up, and one or two months before I was to go back to Japan, Mr. Eto asked if I would like to go on a trip. He took me to Sacramento to see a rice refinement business, the American counterpart of my family's business. On the way, he asked if I had seen Yosemite. I had not, so Mr. Eto took me there for

Mr. Masaji Eto, left, and I at Yosemite in 1963.

my first visit. At that time, you could still drive through the tunnel of the giant sequoia, the Wawona Tree. My backache just disappeared when I saw it. I asked some tourists to stretch their arms around the tree, but there weren't enough of them to all join hands. I asked three more people to join, and they connected hands all the way around. The thick bark on the 2000-year-old tree was beautiful! I was impressed with the age of the tree.

I still like to go to Yosemite and want to share the place with other people. Later in life, when my family and I went to Yosemite, we drove through the tree, but the tree was struck with lightning a few years later and fell. I have always been amazed at the big scale of the United States' nature. The splendor of nature just attached to my brain.

My life on the Eto farm was very hard, but I wanted to keep living in the United States. Now that Chieko was married, I had no reason to want to be in Japan. In June 1963, three months before my departure for Japan, I went to the Japanese Consulate General in Los Angeles to ask how I would be able to return to the United States. I was told that I would need to fill out an application, but that if I had a special skill like Japanese gardening or making tofu, I would have a much better chance to come back to the United States. So, their advice was to get a marketable skill. The workers did not smile and were very cold sending me away with: "Do you have any further questions?"

Before I left to return to Japan, many people had *Soobetsu-kai* 送別会 (going away party) parties for me, and all my Japanese roommates were invited to the parties. At this point, there was nothing definite about whether I would be able to return to the United States.

The first party held for me was at Mr. Sakamoto's home at the camp on Mr. Eto's property. By this time, Mr. Sakamoto was married with children and did not have to pay rent. He was earning $1.25 an hour. George Fukunaga, an owner of a strawberry field, hosted the second party, and his party was held at Mei Hung Low's restaurant in San Luis Obispo. George's wife, his second, was the sister of the second Eto. Mrs. Kumabe hosted the third party. At that time the Kumabe family were living in a house on the property, too, and their son became a professional in the medical field.

The final party was at Mr. Eto's. The second Eto had seven sisters all of whom were married and living away, but four of them came to the party. The first Mrs. Eto also attended the party. At least thirty people attended this party including my roommates. I had a hard time to hold back tears when the American people hugged me at the party. Privately, I cried. The party was a few days before I left, and I wasn't working during that time. I had time to go out and buy one suitcase and an over the shoulder bag for my trip back to Japan.

I had known for a few months that Chieko had married, so I was not interested in returning to Japan. I liked my life in the United States even though my life was very hard. I noticed that people in the United States work on Saturday and Sunday, and I thought that I was strong enough to compete with this hard work. I thought sooner or later I would have an opportunity to live as an average American.

I was to leave right after lunch on September 17, 1963. Mr. and Mrs. Kumabe, Mr. and Mrs. Eto, and Mr. and Mrs. Sakamoto saw me off at the station. I had a signature album, so I know everyone who was there. I was going to take a bus to San Francisco, and at that that time, the Greyhound bus station was in front of the Court House in San Luis Obispo near the Fremont Theater. Sometime into the bus trip, I fell asleep and lost my wallet with $150 in cash. I noticed it was missing just as I got off the bus when the driver was checking seats. I pointed out where I had been sitting, but the driver hadn't seen anything. I lost everything, and it was a great deal of money. Ultimately, someone sent the wallet to the Eto camp, but the money was missing. The younger Japanese workers sent my wallet to me.

I stayed two nights at the Miyako hotel before boarding the ship. I had lost my wallet, but fortunately, through the Tan-no Club, everything had been prepaid for the trip back to Japan, including the hotel stay. The ship I took on the Ellerman's Wilson Line was huge. I took this ship because the Tan-no Club bought many tickets for those traveling between Japan and the United States at a reduced cost. It was much cheaper than for those not in the club. The Japanese government supported this organization in the hope that students could make use of it and learn useful information for Japanese farmers. Later it was called an internship. It cost $40.00 a year to be a member of the Tan-no Club, and twice a year we meet in LA to eat dinner together. At one time our branch had fifty-nine members, but now, there are only a few people left. Students and farmers would come from Japan during the summer to learn how to mechanize farming. Nowadays, there is not too much benefit to them to come to the United States. The only concern in California is the Colorado River running dry. In Japan, winter is an issue for agriculture, and farmers must build greenhouses. Some people still come here to study fruit and vegetable growing methods, but in the United States, pears are mass-produced, and in Japan, pears are wrapped individually on the tree, and they grow very large.

On the ship, I was excited to experience the Pacific Ocean. This was the first time to see with my own eyes that the earth is round, and we were able to tell that within several minutes there would be rain because we could see the complete sky. But because I become seasick easily, I was told to always look at the horizon, limiting what I could look at. In terms of seasickness, the first three days were the hardest: we were told not to look down and not to look at the Golden Gate Bridge. I wanted to see the bridge so badly that I held my hand over my eyes and peeked through my fingers. I was lying down on my back because standing my body swayed more and made me more prone to seasickness. Many days passed without seeing any other vessel on the water, but one day there was an announcement that a ship was coming. As we were passing it in the Pacific, we all went on deck and waved. Americans on my ship were going to Japan for a vacation. Every night they dressed and danced. I only peeked through the windows because I didn't have a suit, so I didn't feel comfortable going in.

The Japanese Tan-no Club people were housed all together. We had the cheapest rooms near the engine, and it was a noisy location and smelled of oil. At least there were no mosquitos, but I was very uncomfortable. I finally took a blanket and slept on the deck. I could eat meals at any time twenty-four hours a day and any amount I wanted, but since I got seasick, I had to be careful. I didn't have a private room; in fact, far from it: there were ten people in the room all sleeping on cots, and we had to share a bathroom and shower.

The ship took seven days to get to Hawaii: we stayed there about twenty-three hours total, but we had only eight hours off the ship. I went to a pineapple farm and bought six pineapples. I wanted to give them to my father, and I immediately had them sent to him in Kumamoto from Hawaii. Chieko's brother, who now worked at the train station, later said he could smell the pineapples through the box. He was curious, so he looked at the return address and saw that the box that smelled like pineapple was from me. He called my father and told him that the pineapples were coming. When the pineapples arrived, my mother put them in front of the Shinto Shrine. Such an unusual food like pineapple is offered to the gods first, and then it is eaten. This is part of tradition: we feel good psychologically following tradition. Then my parents shared the pineapple with our relatives: real pineapple from Hawaii! Meanwhile, after another seven days, we arrived in Yokohama, Japan. The cruise was only a little pleasure because I was deeply concerned about my future life: Chieko could not be mine; I wanted to return to the United States.

Five

Return to Japan

I stayed in Japan for two years and ten months. During this time in Japan, I was preparing to return to the United States by learning the art of landscaping so that my expired visa could be renewed. By this time, I had a definite plan to return to the United States.

Disappointment

1963–1965

I was twenty-six years old when I returned to Japan via ship. There was an announcement at 6:00 a.m. on the day we arrived in Japan that we would be able to see the Japanese Isles. This was my first time to see Japan from the outside; Mt. Fuji was not visible because of the fog. I did not feel happiness to see Japan because I was thinking about how I could get back to the United States.

In *atotsugi* 跡継ぎ (heir or successor), a Japanese tradition, the oldest son is responsible for the care of the parents and takes over the family name and responsibilities. He inherits everything. So traditionally and because I am the oldest son capable of carrying on the hard labor of the family business, I should be the child to take care of my parents and to take over the family name and responsibilities. My elder half-brother was not able to take over because when he went to war, he was shot in the leg and left with an injury that prevented him from doing the heavy work of carrying heavy 60 kg. bags of rice. My half-brother was fifteen years older than I with three children and a wife. For a while, they were living with us, and at one point, thirteen people lived in our house, with one bathroom.

When I returned to Japan from the United States after three years, I believed I had a better chance at success in the United States because there was a great economic gap between the United States and Japan. When I told my parents that I was returning to the United States, they were disappointed that I was going to leave. But I felt that since there were seven children, at least one child should try his luck in the United States. We didn't believe that the family business was going to boom, but my parents knew that I was cautious in business, so they were disappointed that I would not oversee the family business. My brothers were more willing to take risks. So, after I told my father that I declined to inherit anything, my father told my brother, Futoru, that *atotsugi* would fall on him. An official paper came to me that I had to sign to give up the right to inherit. When I came to the United States for the first time under the three-year contract, my parents' second son, Futoru, was given the responsibility. Futoru became a city councilman at twenty-three years old. When he ran in the city election, I sent him enough money for his campaign, which delayed the purchase of my own home by three years. Ultimately, Futoru failed in business and lost everything.

When I was in the United States, my mother's deceased sister's son had asked me if I could give him 50,000 yen ($139) (the exchange rate at that time was 360 yen to the dollar) so that he could get his truck driver's license. I sent him the money he needed so that he would be able to have a stable income. When I returned to Japan, I stayed with this older half-brother in Chiba-ken. I had become used to some of the luxuries in the United States that I did not have in Japan. I was unhappy when I returned and found things had not changed in Japan.

My half-brother had an old-fashioned bathroom that smelled, and there were worms down in the toilet; I was very disgusted by that.

Before I left Japan, I had thought my family's house was large and most people considered it large, but after having been in the United States, I noticed how low the ceilings were and how dark the house was. The old-fashioned bathroom and low ceilings bothered me after having experienced modern America. In the United States and on the cruise ship, I had been able to eat as much as I wanted, but back in Japan it was only rice, daikon, fish, and soup: no meat. My diet was changed drastically. When I returned to Japan after three years in the United States, I noticed that paper napkins looked smaller, and people looked skinnier. People moved like little ants, very fast, here and there: they didn't move with confidence.

My half-brother wanted to take me to Nikko where the tomb that contained Tokugawa-shogun's bones is located, but the road to get there was terrible. Driving down the road with my brother, I noticed that the road was narrow and had many toll booths slowing up traffic unlike the United States' broad roads. You couldn't just drive freely as you could on the broad American road: it was start and stop, and the cars could barely pass. I was shocked by the narrowness of the road. I was seated between my brother and his wife: as we drove, I became carsick, and finally they stopped the truck, and I threw up in newspaper while my sister-in-law pounded my back. It was a three-and-a-half-hour drive.

When I saw Nikko Toshogu, I was not moved very much, but when I went back many years later, I was very moved. My heart didn't have enough space during my first visit because I was busy thinking about my future, but during the second visit, my heart and mind were more relaxed, and I had enough space in my heart to observe and appreciate the details.

Homecoming! Banzai!

I had not been to my parental home in Kyushu since returning to Japan, so after a while, I decided it was time to go home. Since my brother had to work, his nephew took me to Tokyo, where I caught the train for my trip home. The trip from Tokyo took seventeen hours. When I arrived in Kumamoto, eleven people met me at Ohmuta train station: seven friends and four of my siblings. From the station, it took forty-five minutes on the back of a bicycle to get to my house. When we arrived, there were forty people waiting to welcome me for a surprise welcome home party.

As I entered the house, my uncle shouted three times, *"Banzai"* 万歳 (live long), and everyone joined in. The guests didn't know, but there was a gap in my emotions and the emotions of the people who were welcoming me. I had returned to Japan knowing that Chieko was married, and I was planning to return to the United States: I didn't feel at all like celebrating. My mother had cried when she saw me; I know she wanted to hug me, but that is not the Japanese way. The guests were all drunk, and manners dictated that I was expected to drink with them, but I don't drink. So, I would touch a drink to my lips and pour it out. It would have been rude if I hadn't accepted an offered drink. Guests were drunk when I arrived after sunset, and they were drunk when the party ended after midnight. My father's drunken friends promised to arrange a marriage for me. I had heard this so many times from so many people, but I was not interested. When everyone had left, I cried with my mother, but my only interest was in returning to the United States.

All the people I ran in to at home were curious about the United States. I told them that food is totally different. I told them that in Japan, we take fruit to a person in the hospital, but in the United States, you can eat fruit, meat, eggs, and milk every day. I told them that even as a worker, I was eating those foods daily. They did not believe me. They thought that only the owner of the farm could eat that well. They thought it a luxury to eat even a morsel of meat every day as they had it only at New Year's or at Obon.

What I didn't tell them, however, was how hard the work had been.

After the guests had left, I couldn't go to sleep because I was so excited. That night, my parents had prepared a futon between them for me because they wanted to hear all my stories. That had never happened before. It was my father's idea to put the futon between my mother and him for me. My father was severe and complained a great deal, but lying there between them was a wonderful feeling. He told me that thanks to my hard work, the debt had been significantly reduced. My father taught me what a relationship is supposed to be between parents and children. My mother wanted to hear more and more about my experiences, so we talked most of the night.

My father had hoped I would remain in Japan. I had been able to return only fifty percent of my father's debt, but my father was extremely happy with how much I had done. Japanese men are so macho that he could not thank me directly, so he told my mother to thank me. She told me that my father was so thankful that he was tearful. He was hardheaded.

At my parents' house, my mother was still cooking the old-fashioned way with wood creating a great deal of smoke. In the United States, I had been using gas to cook. And I was surprised that it was still common in the area to use a pump to get water. In the *benjo* 便所 (toilet), I had to squat and tolerate the smell. I didn't want any of it. For three years in the United States, I hadn't experienced this; I could feel I was going to have a hard time readjusting. It took about one month to adjust to the benjo: I missed the flush toilet, and for the first few weeks, I was very disgusted. (Now, I don't like the high-tech toilets in Japan that spray water to clean the bottom because when the water hits me, I jump.)

I didn't say anything, of course, about my dissatisfactions with Japan. Everyone would have thought I was stuck up, and they would have called me a liar about American conveniences. In the United States I had found hot water coming out of the shower and a clean gas stove very convenient. I felt Japan was very behind; Mr. Eto had told me that Japan was two decades behind at that time.

The custom in Japan is to greet neighbors with a gift when you return from having been abroad. Villages were divided into sections, and the smallest unit was the homes near one family's house which made a *rinpou-gumi* 隣保組, a division determined hundreds of years ago during the feudal period. If anyone in this group had a funeral, for example, all people in the rinpoo-gumi would provide food, and the family would not have to cook. The rinpoo-gumi included six houses to the right, six to the left, and sometimes the houses across the street. I said, *"Osewani narimashita"* お世話になりました, ("I am back and thank you for having taken care of my family."). After saying, "Osewani narimashita," relatives in the rinpoo-gumi would invite me to supper to hear more stories about the Unites States since it was rare for anyone to go to a foreign country. I repeated the same stories over and over. I took three bars of Hersey's chocolate to each family. In the end, I went beyond the rinpoo-gumi and visited fourteen families: I was a star. To my uncles and aunts, I talked more about the hardships, but to my judo group, I talked about the prostitutes. I would go with the judo group to get udon and talk. They asked me many questions including how I liked blond girls. I looked forward to these talks at the udon shops.

Mitsui Miiki Coal Mine Disaster

November 9, 1963, between my first and second trips to the US, four hundred fifty-eight people died in the Mitsui Miiki Coal Mine disaster, and all but twenty died of carbon monoxide poisoning. Another eight hundred thirty-three people were injured. I heard about miners who had been exposed to the carbon monoxide and had lived, but many were left with severe and permanent brain damage.

Half an hour or so before the explosion, my friend, Mitsuo Mabuchi, and I had gone to the coal mine in his three-wheeled car because I wanted to see the mine. He stayed in the car while I went to investigate. After looking at the entrance and surrounding area, I returned to the car. Just as I opened the door and my friend started the engine, at that very moment, there was an explosion that shook the car and everything around it. A gigantic blast of smoke came gushing out of the mine.

We ran away at first, but we quickly realized help was needed. Initially we couldn't do anything because there was still a great deal of smoke coming out. A siren was blaring. It was a different sound from the wartime sirens, which were a fast, high-pitched sound from a bell being struck. The siren we were hearing on this day was the one used by the fire department. The first wave of miners who had been in the mine but near the outside, were running and holding their heads and faces, which were totally covered with black coal dust. People who came out in the next wave had their clothes burned. Many who came out suddenly lost consciousness and fell. Their eyes, mouths, and ears were all filled with coal, but some of these men of the first and second wave survived. Their noses were packed full of tiny pieces of coal. They couldn't breathe because of the coal in their noses, so we took hashi and dug out the coal to allow them to breathe. All the nearby neighbors came to help. People weren't able to recognize their relatives, so they took wet towels and wiped faces clean to help with identification. My friend and I had arrived about 2:00 p.m. and stayed until 4:00 a.m. the next morning. I didn't eat anything during this time or even think about eating.

Finding a Profession and Finding a Wife

SPRING LIGHT GARDEN

For the first six months after my return to Kumamoto, I was talking with friends and working about three or four hours a day in the family business refining rice, but in the meantime, my father and uncles repeatedly said that I should get married. I said that I didn't want to get married because I planned to return to the United States. Because I had learned at the consulate in Los Angeles that I would have to have a special skill to return to the United States, I decided to apply to a landscape company to learn landscaping. I didn't like the idea making of tofu because the work seemed too feminine. I preferred physical labor.

My brothers already had jobs, so I didn't have a great deal of pressure to look for work. My father was not happy about my leaving again for the United States, but I convinced him that maybe it would be helpful for one out of seven children to go.

When the New Year began, I had been accepted into a landscaping company, and I started learning landscaping. Mr. Tadashi Yoshimura owned the Skunkoen Company: "Spring Light Garden." He had an associate who was his wife's younger brother, Mr. Susumu. He had been working for Mr. Yoshimura for thirty years, and he was paid $1,000 a month: a very fine salary. I was an apprentice to Yoshimura for one year and eight months. I was only paid a minimal amount because I was learning, but this connection gave me an opportunity to meet my wife, Faith.

Normally a student works under a master landscaper for fifteen years. During this time, landscaping secrets are not shared, and the trainee must just dig holes and be a gofer. The first three years are usually a test to see if the apprentice can be patient and last. If he is really devoted, the teacher will teach him something. The student carries dirt, rocks, and gravel, and the master tells him where to place them. The student can design nothing and is expected to listen and learn.

When there were no garden design jobs, we shaped wealthy people's tall pines. We had three-legged ladders, and to stabilize them, we connected the top of the ladder to the tree with ropes. We had to remove excess needles without gloves because pruning the needles was a delicate process. By the end of the day, our hands were swollen. I soaked my hands in lukewarm water, but when I took a hot bath, I had to keep my hands out of the water because they stung so badly.

Traditional teachers like mine don't teach anything for three years, but my teacher knew that I had a plan to go back to the United States, so he began to teach me immediately. The first thing I learned was how to move a very large rock from the street to the back yard. There was no machine to help lift or move the rock, and we had to move it without disturbing people or fences. To move the rock, we rolled it over metal pipes with wood under them. After a certain distance was gained, the pipes were moved to the front, and the stone was again rolled over the pipes.

I had an opportunity to go with my master, Mr. Yoshimura, to the home of the head of the Mayors' Association of Japan where I saw an incredible garden. My master had designed and finished the front garden and had been hired to design and implement the design for the back yard; my job was to move rocks and plant plants. Mr. Yoshimura had an extremely devoted work ethic. He would look and look at a stone or plant and have me move it an inch to the left or right, dig again, and once again move the entire thing. My workday was from 8:00 to 5:00. Even though there were two of us working for him, Susumu and I, the entire eight hours might be devoted to positioning a rock, maybe two. I simply stood waiting until the boss made a decision. I thought that I should clean something as I waited, but when I began, he told me not to disturb his concentration. My thinking that I was wasting time was the American way of thinking, but Mr. Yoshimura was making a very important decision. For four hours he was looking for the correct position; he was evaluating by moving things around and looking from different angles and varying distances. Susumu had had many years to get used to this. I thought that this patience might be the reason why Japanese gardens are considered art. He was considering how to place a waterfall, trees, and rocks; I thought this must be very difficult. Nothing is linear in Japanese gardening: there is no symmetry. In eight hours, we might position two rocks. I didn't get bored even though we moved the rocks only about six or seven times. Yoshimura said to just give him time, and I tried to understand his concern. I had thought that a gardener's job was to plant, but I began to think that the gardener is really an artist. I was convinced that I really liked landscaping, and I was charmed with gardening.

Susumu and I enjoyed talking, and after a while, he had asked me why I wanted to learn landscaping, and I told him that I needed a special skill so that I might eventually return to the United States. We enjoyed talking so much that he invited me to his house so we could talk more. I went and as we talked, Susumu asked me if I had seen a girl who had just walked by. I said that I had not, and that I was not interested in women because I wanted to go to the United States. But Susumu persisted and told me about this girl's background. He told me that she was a United States citizen. My eyes opened widely: I thought that if I married this girl, I didn't have to have a special skill or license, and that I could go back to America tomorrow. He went on to tell me that she had been born in Hawaii, but her grandparents, with whom she and her mother lived, wanted to die in Kumamoto. The young woman planned to return to the United States and live in California after the death of her grandparents. And on top of all of that, it turned out that she was a far relative of my master, Yoshimura, and Mr. Susumu was a nephew of her grandparents!

I asked him to introduce me to her, and he introduced her as Faith.

I determined I would ask her out her: she was twenty-two, and I was twenty-eight.

STRUGGLE TO GET THE GIRL

When I asked Faith to go to a restaurant with me, she said that she was too busy. I tried anther day, and she again said that she was too busy. The third time, I told her that I would go to the restaurant and wait for her. So, I went and waited: after about ten minutes when I was just about to order for myself, I noticed a pretty girl coming. I had thought the pretty girl was someone else, not the girl who had been introduced to me as Faith, because she had done up her hair and had a pretty dress on and was wearing lipstick.

But it was Faith, and when she sat down, I said, "Let's eat. What do you want?" I knew that she was very nervous because she was drinking water all the time. I was nervous, too, because I had never taken a girl to dinner. I didn't know what to say, but I paid. At least I knew that I had to do that. I asked her if she wanted to look around, but she said that she had to go home. I asked if she would meet me the next Saturday, and she said she might. She was hard to get, very hard. I was wiping sweat off in the effort.

Later, when she finally agreed to go out with me again, I took her for a ride in a Mazda-minette, a three wheeled car. I took her in this car to Kumamoto castle, parked the car, and we talked. We did not go far enough to make a baby, but Faith and I were kissing at the castle. A policeman came and shined a flashlight on us, but he left immediately without saying anything. His partner came back, apologized for interrupting, and very politely asked us to leave because it was closing time. It turns out the first policeman was a judoist, Mr. Ozaki, and he recognized me. He got his partner to tell me to leave because it would have been impolite to tell me, an older judoist, to leave.

Faith, twenty-one years old.

Finally, some weeks later, we did go far enough to create a baby, and after knowing her for two months, she was pregnant. When I heard the news that she was pregnant, I felt totally committed, and she was calm and prepared. My father had told me since I was old enough to be told, that I should not have sex unless I was married. If you were to have sex, he said, do not tell a lie. The worst thing for me to do would be to have sex and lie about it. But it didn't matter anyway because we were leaving Japan. My wife was two months pregnant when we went to the consulate in Fukuoka, and the consulate employees recommended that we marry that day, so we did. We then had to go to the American Consulate to fill out the form for marriage and were then sent to City Hall. Meanwhile, the American Consulate prepared the paperwork. I didn't know how to fill the forms, so my wife filled them out in a few minutes. I was amazed at how well she did this and realized that the fact that she could read and write English was a great gain.

After ten days, we returned to the Consulate and City Hall. The paperwork had been completed at both places and the marriage was official. By the time of the civil ceremony, Faith was about three months pregnant. Our son was born on April 25, 1966.

GETTING MARRIED

Faith and I had a wedding celebration in a *ryokan* 旅館 (traditional Japanese inn) about one month after the civil ceremony. My wife's family and friends chartered a bus, and in all, we had about thirty-five people in attendance. The number of guests from my family was restricted because more people would have cost more than we could afford. My judo teacher, who was invited but couldn't attend the wedding celebration, sent a message of congratulations.

I had thought that we would have to stay at home for our honeymoon because we didn't have enough money. I had to prepare money to come to the United States, which was going to cost 320,000 ¥ (about $890) for two on Pan American Airlines one-way. Since I didn't have enough money for a honeymoon, my best friend, Mr. Takashira, made and paid for a reservation for two nights at the Shirasagi-so Hotel Hot Springs for us. It was his present. Mr. Takashira had told the guests to bring cash rather than gifts. The guests did bring money, and we used the money to cover the cost of the wedding celebration. I wore a *hakama* 袴 (traditional clothing, skirt-like pants) and *montsuki* 紋付 (a Japanese kimono used for formal occasions) with my family seal. Faith wore a kimono with a traditional wig. Our wedding day was a day of heavy rain. An old superstition says that if a man likes to eat the half-burned rice stuck to the bottom of the pot, there will be a heavy rain on his wedding day. My older sister reminded me that since I was a little boy I had liked to eat the half-burned rice.

At that time, after the wedding, a husband walked three meters ahead of his wife, and they never walked arm in arm. The groom was expected to carry all the *furoshiki* 風呂敷 (traditional cloth for wrapping) for the honeymoon. The honeymoon was usually two nights and three days, and the couple would return home in the dark because they were embarrassed. If they rode in the three-wheeled car, they could snuggle, and the groom could even kiss the bride because they were seated close enough.

My childhood sweetheart, Chieko, was married. Before I left the first time, I had told her that three years was too long for her to wait for me. Two years after my return to the United States with Faith, she heard that I had married. She told my best friend, Mr. Takashira, that she was hurt that I had not let her know that I was going to be married. She had wanted to hear from me that I was going to get married. At that time, divorce was very rare, so when people got married, it was for life. Marriage was a very serious matter.

When my father's banker friend, Mr. Ooishi, he heard that I was ready to go to the United States, he was impressed because he knew how hard the work was. Mr. Ooishi had gone to the United States in 1902 to Guadalupe, California, with his brother as farm laborers. After eight years, Mr. Ooishi gave up because the work was too hard, but his brother stayed in the United States and made a great success. Ultimately, the brother owned a department store in Los Angeles; he has since died, and now his third generation owns it. Mr. Ooishi returned to Japan and started a credit union. He told my father that knowing how hard the work is, and if your son is going back, that he could arrange for me to borrow money. Mr. Ooishi asked me if I were serious about returning to the United States. He said that he knew a man who would sign a loan so that I could borrow some money. Later, when I was just about ready to leave Japan, I did borrow 320,000 ¥ ($890).

LESSONS OF GRANDPARENTS AND SUSUMU

My wife had lived with her grandparents for twelve years. By the time we were married, her grandparents were living in Japan. Faith's grandparents had immigrated to Hawaii and then retired to their hometown in Japan because of the strength of the dollar: one dollar was equal to 360 yen. Their American social security monthly income converted to yen equaled 85,000 yen or $236. At that time, a university professor's salary was 20,000 yen per month or $56, and a company president was earning about 40,000 yen per month or $111. They had a nice house, and I wondered how they could live without working, and this was the answer.

When Faith lived in Hawaii, she graduated from an American high school. On Sundays, while she was attending the American high school and continuing after graduation, she went to a Japanese high school and was able to graduate at twenty-one. Her mother was a *nisei* 二世 (second generation) and had been born in Hawaii. When my wife was in the fifth grade, her parents divorced. Her mother, she, and Faith's grandparents all lived together.

The location of my work was about forty miles from my own home, so Faith and I were invited to stay at Faith's grandparents, which was nearby my work and just a short bicycle ride. Faith's grandparents had a large house, and they let Susumu and his wife live on one side of the house. Susumu's parents wouldn't let him and his family live with them because they were against Susumu's marriage.

Susumu loved *shochu* 焼酎, a strong potato-based sake, and he drank two glasses every day. I thought it was a wonder that he wasn't killed because when he was drunk: he would ride his bicycle very fast. When he was drunk, he began complaining about things, and he talked to his wife in a very nasty way. Susumu and his wife fought just about every day, and because we were all living in the same house, I could clearly hear them. The argument would continue until Faith's grandfather intervened. Faith's grandparents were used to hearing the daily arguing, but it was a new experience for me to hear a couple fight every night. I was wondering if this is the way for married couples.

Susumu was a humble and quiet man until he became drunk. Even though his wife was a strong woman and fought back, he was violent and hit her. The first time I heard him being violent was quite shocking to me. Faith's grandparents told Susumu's wife to keep her mouth shut when Susumu was drinking, and he would go to sleep. Faith's grandparents also told Susumu to drink just a small amount because he couldn't hold his liquor. The neighbors knew that he was a quiet and gentle man, and even they told him not to drink because he normally was like a Buddha.

Susumu and his wife never did divorce, and his wife died in 2013. I had thought he would die first because of his drinking. The last time I saw him, he was bent over and looked so old.

When Faith and I awakened at her grandparents' house, breakfast was ready, and Faith's grandmother would pack my lunch. I would get home from work by 5:00 p.m., and I didn't always wait for Faith to come home from her bookkeeping job to eat because I was hungry. Faith's grandmother was a good cook, and she had callouses where she held a knife. I liked her very much, and since I was the husband to her granddaughter, I was treated like an emperor. Faith's grandfather was quiet, but her grandmother was talkative: she was in charge of everything, so the grandfather was lazy. He went fishing because he had nothing else to do. Her grandmother's social security was much more than her grandfather's, and I thought that the grandmother's financial strength was a big mistake because the grandfather lost authority, and he was defensive about that. She would tell him to get out of her way; he could do what he wanted as long as he didn't get in her hair.

Because they were well off, Faith's grandparents had a nineteen-inch black and white television. Up to fifteen neighbors would come to watch TV at a time, and Faith's grandmother would feed all of them. Neighbors, for their part, came with rice and vegetables and fruit. During a sumo tournament, the neighbors would come for fifteen days straight.

Every Sunday, Faith's mother and grandmother went to a hot spring. Faith and I would take a twenty-minute ride by bicycle to downtown Kumamoto. We would walk together on the major streets, have lunch, and go window-shopping. It was a happy time, and I wanted to stay at her grandparents' home as long as possible because I was spoiled.

Faith's mother's job was to spend money and enjoy herself. She was always out; sometimes she was gone four or five days a week travelling with her many friends. She was a pleasant person, but I didn't respect her. Faith and I were ready to start our new life, and her mother had plenty of money, but she showed no interest in supporting us in

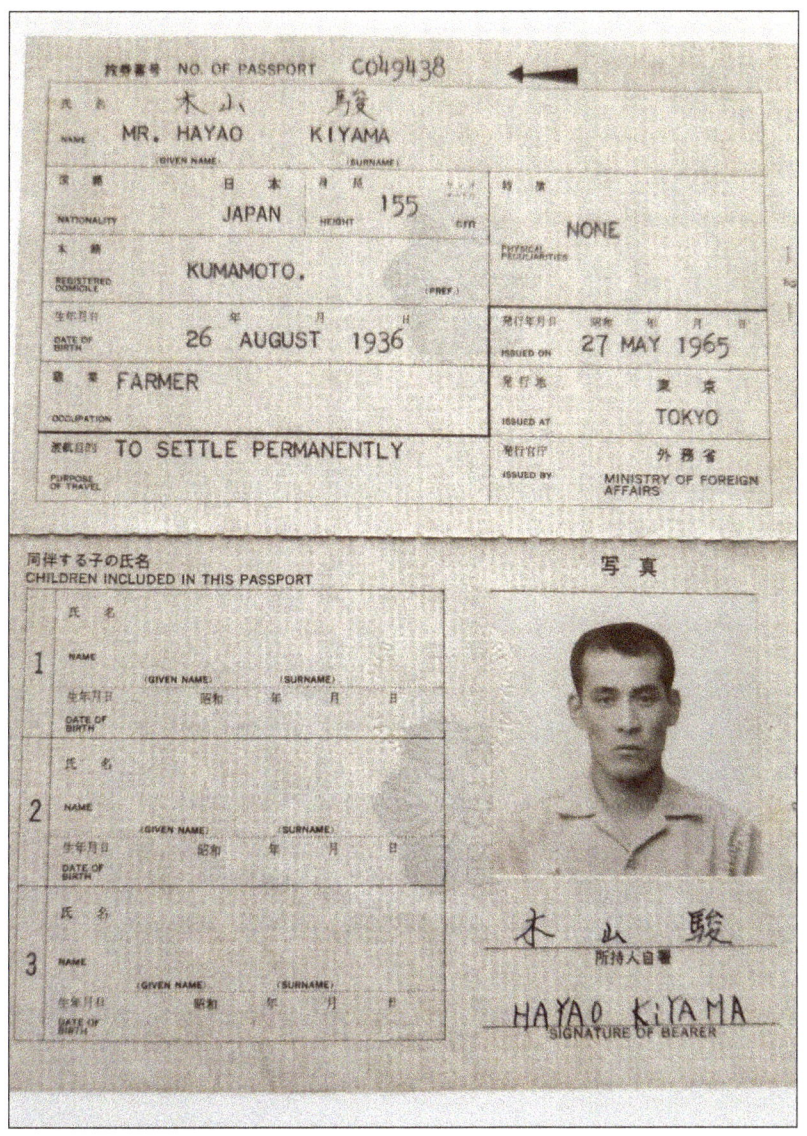

The inside of my passport.

our new life. Her mother was born in America, so she didn't have the Japanese value system to sacrifice for her children, and on top of that, she never worked. In fact, she didn't know how to work, so I knew that when the grandparents died, her cash from them would stop, and Faith's mother would have no way to survive. I was aware she would be in trouble. So, when they did die, I said it was better for Faith's mother to inherit all of the money. She sold the house to Susumu, and he remodeled and continued to live there.

I asked Faith's grandparents if Faith could stay with them for three months, and then after I settled in the United States, I would call for her to join me. They didn't think it was a good idea; they thought we should share the hardship of starting a new life. They said, "Just go." Now I understand what they meant and think their idea was the right one. I agreed immediately, but I felt sorry for Faith as she was pregnant, and I had no money. Before Faith and I left, we had two farewell parties: one at Faith's grandparents and one at my home. At my parents' party, people were talking to me, but my mind was on the future, and I heard very little.

TRANSITIONING

In September 1965, my wife, Faith, and I left from Hanada Airport for the United States, via Hawaii, on a Pan American flight. We spent five days in Hawaii with extended family members and Faith's grandparents' friends. Every day was a feast. The first morning that I awakened, I was astonished with the greenness of Hawaii and the brilliant sun. We went sight-seeing in Honolulu, and we visited a pineapple farm where we ate incredibly sweet pineapple. But my mind was on our new life in the United States. I was concerned about the arrival of the baby because I wanted to provide Faith and the baby with a quiet lifestyle. We no longer had Faith's grandparents around as support, so I was rather more worried about having a baby than looking forward to it. The baby started kicking, and Faith's tight stomach made me even more aware of the coming baby.

In Hawaii, my wife's relatives gave us money gifts: $85.00. That plus the $25 cash in American money I still had with me from my first tour of work was the foundation cash for us to start a life in the United States: $110. My wife's father, who was in Los Angeles, had sent cash for me to buy a suit that could be used for any formal occasion, so I had bought a suit before I left Japan. My master had said he would write a landscaping certificate for me, but he never did. If I were going to return to the United States alone, then a certificate would have been evidence that I was an immigrant with a special skill, but the fact that my wife was an American citizen was much more powerful than a certificate.

LOS ANGELES BEFORE THE NEXT REALITY

Finally, it was time to leave Hawaii, and we flew from Honolulu to Los Angeles. My wife's father and her stepmother were at the airport to welcome us. I stayed about one week with them and then took a bus to Mr. Eto's farm in Los Osos, CA, because we needed my work income, but Faith stayed three months longer. I was eager to make money because the baby was coming. A small prefab house was being assembled at Mr. Eto's, and when it was completed, Faith would join me.

Faith's father was a carpenter; he was also a drinker. He drank every night, and he started drinking at 10: 00 p.m. But he was a quiet man whose attitude was to stay calm and take your time: decide slowly and carefully, and I believe that my wife took after him in that regard. Faith, like her father, is the type of person who takes things as they come. Even now she doesn't complain about hardships. When something is painful, I express the pain, but she doesn't unless she is asked.

Faith's mother was an only child, so her father became a *yoshi* 婿養子 (man adopted into family by marriage and takes family name). Since her mother was an only child and a girl, he changed his last name to her last name so that the family name could be carried on. When Faith's father came into the family as a yoshi, her grandmother, who had plenty of money from her successful restaurant, treated him as a welcomed guest. She told him to take it easy, and that he had no responsibilities. So, he went to drinking places every night, and that is where he met his second wife. My wife was born after her parents had been married ten years. Her brother was born seven years after her birth. Faith was eight years old when her father left.

I told Faith that once we reached the United States, life would be difficult, but that the hard life wouldn't last forever. She is very skilled at the abacus and had worked for a small business as a bookkeeper. With her grandparents' support and her job, she had been well off. But since I knew that we wouldn't have much in the United States, I asked Faith to prepare all necessities that she could. I tried hard to convince Faith that the first ten or fifteen years in the United States were going to be very difficult, but I also promised her that life would get better. I thought it was better to tell her before she saw the reality. My emphasis was on the fact that it would not be for her full life: I told her it would be fifteen years at the most, and that I would take responsibility. She was quite down when I told her about the hardships, but she was already pregnant so there was no backing out. When she arrived at the Eto property, her pregnancy was clearly visible. She was absolutely shaken when she saw where we would

My house on the Eto property. When I visited my former house on the Eto farm in 2008, it looked like a jungle of trees were taking over the house. My eyes watered; I hadn't thought about this place for years. Some people were living there with two dogs, and I was afraid of being bitten. I lived in that house five years from 1965–1970. We had a septic tank, and once a year a pump truck would come to pump it out. I was really near the threshold psychologically when we lived there. Even though it was a very hard time, I now have a melancholy feeling about the time I spent there. The Japanese word for the way I felt is natsukashii 懐かしい (nostalgia); *there is no corresponding word in English. The distinction between life then and now is what causes the feeling of natsukashii in me. Some of my best memories include my children's birthday parties and coming home from work and the three children were playing in the dirt digging holes or a tunnel. There were no video games for my kids to play at that time, so they dug holes. When they saw me coming come, they came running yelling, "Daddy! Daddy!"*

be living; she noticed that we didn't own a car, and there were only fields outside our small home.

There was no television, no stores, no shops; there was nothing. She was convinced of what I had told her, and she could tell that her disappointment made me feel down: this was my reality. I continued to repeat that the hardship wouldn't last a full life: it would end. I think Faith was in love with me, otherwise she would have left before we were married. I was near the edge because I had to repeatedly tell her it wouldn't last forever; I felt an unexpectedly strong responsibility for my words.

My father had told me that when you are young and are having a hard time, extra energy comes. Simply meet the hardship, and you can count on the extra energy. His advice was perfectly correct. Before complaining about your situation, just start working. Don't analyze, don't look for reasons, just work. Because of my family responsibilities, I decided not to put unnecessary things in my body: no cigarettes or alcohol, and because I could not afford to be sick, I ate only healthful foods.

Six

Returning to the Farm with a Pregnant Wife

A Farm Worker's Family Life 1966–1970

HUSBAND, WIFE, CHILDREN, AND EARNING A LIVING

I had returned to the United States for a second tour at Mr. Eto's farm with a pregnant wife.

The day after I arrived at the Eto farm, at age 28, I began to work; I thought about nothing but work. I didn't have enough money to rent an apartment. Before Faith joined me at the Eto farm, I was sleeping at the camp where I had stayed during my first three years at the Eto farm. So, while Mr. Eto was having the prefabricated house assembled for us that had a refrigerator and a toilet, it was not yet ready. Faith didn't want to be separated for too long, so she came before the house was ready and stayed with Mr. and Mrs. Sakamoto for a few weeks, next to where our house would be. There was a welcoming party for her when she arrived, but life for Faith went from better to worse.

The Eto's built two small prefab houses, but we had no furniture in ours, so Faith and I used two wooden lettuce boxes as a table and sat on the floor to eat. Since we had no zabutons, we made them out of blankets that Mrs. Sakamoto and Mrs. Kumabe had given us. We also had no bed, but Mrs. Eto said that she would buy a new bed for herself and Mr. Eto, and that Faith I could use their twenty-five-year-old king-sized bed. It was still usable; we were in a sort of camping situation. The prefab house we lived in had electricity and a large butane gas tank, and the $.80 an hour I earned included the house, electricity, and gas. The house looked as if it were made of pressed wood: it had one bedroom, one bathroom, and one room that served as the kitchen, dining, and living room. We did have screens on the windows. Mrs. Eto offered that when the baby was born, she would take Faith and the baby for well-baby checkups; Mrs. Eto was very kind to Faith.

After a couple of days living in the prefab house together, I asked Faith to make miso soup. When I returned home from work that day, she was crying; she didn't know how to make miso soup. My wife had been raised in a comfortable family, and she had never learned to cook. Her grandmother had done everything for her, so I taught her how to make miso soup. She was, however, studying a book on the care of babies that she had brought from Japan, and she did clean and wash dishes. But I think it was the first time she had ever washed dishes, because she did not get the dishes clean.

Our first baby, Jeffery, was born at Sierra Vista hospital in San Luis Obispo; three days after his birth, Mrs. Eto said that after my work she would take me to see my baby. I wished I could have been with Faith to witness the birth, but I was driving a tractor. I cried when I was working; I wanted to see my baby, but I couldn't afford to miss work because it would mean less money. So, on the day of his birth, Mrs. Eto came to my place and told me it was a healthy baby, and everything was going well.

Three days later, Mrs. Eto took me to the hospital, and when I went to the nursery, there were six babies in the nursery. The nurse noticed that I was the only Asian, so she carried my son to the window. My first thought was that he was a beautiful baby, and the second thought involved my responsibilities. Faith and I looked through the glass. I cried when I held my baby, but I did not cry for the second and third babies. I cried again when Jo Anne, my only daughter, was born because my dream to have a daughter had come true. It took two extra children to get a daughter.

Mrs. Eto was very kind and generous and took over like a grandmother, and she behaved similarly for all the Japanese families. But the Eto's were careful with money. When Mr. Eto was forty-eight years old, he chaperoned his daughter's high school graduation trip to Disneyland. This was his first visit there, and it didn't cost him anything.

When Jeffery came home from the hospital, I used the following method to help my wife. The baby was crying all night because he was hungry: no milk was coming from my wife's breasts. I couldn't go to Mrs. Eto, because she would have said to take my wife to the doctor, and I didn't have money to take her to the doctor. But I did have a memory of my grandmother taking gauze in the shape of a nipple, dipping it into sugar water, and giving it to the baby. I did that for Jeffery, and it helped temporarily. My wife's breasts were tight, and she was in pain. I used a warm moist towel with a gentle massage for a while, dipping the towel in warm water and wringing it out. When that didn't work, I fell on one of her breasts to try to loosen the milk. She screamed in pain, and then rotten milk came out. I wiped it off and fresh milk appeared, and then I did it again to the other breast and rotten milk came out again, and then fresh milk came. The pain left, and she was relieved.

Because I had observed the care of my younger siblings, I was somewhat prepared to have children. I had learned to use my elbow to test the water for a baby's bath. But when it was time to give Jeffery a bath, I accidentally scratched his belly button area with my long fingernails and blood came gushing out. The fingernail had torn off the umbilical cord, and in my underwear, I ran to the Eto's because there was so much blood, and I thought I had killed my own baby. He had lost so much blood that I think he was in shock. Mrs. Eto said there was no need to take the baby to the doctor, and all that I needed to do was put petroleum jelly on the cord area. I had lots of opportunity to get better at taking care of children as we went on to have three more.

Three of my children were born during the second Eto work tour. The hospital bill for the birth of the first baby was $750.00. The cost of the second baby's birth was $950.00, and the third, $1180.00. For each of these three births, Mrs. Eto told us not to worry, that she would cover the cost as a loan. I was being paid $450.00 a month, and Mrs. Eto asked how much should be taken out of my salary to cover the hospital bills. I said either $20.00 or $30.00. I never had $50.00 removed at one time because money was tight, so I returned money borrowed for my son's birth through the installment plan. After our third son was born, all five of us slept in one room. I slept on the floor and Faith and the children slept on the king-sized bed Mr. and Mrs. Eto had given us. Faith just tried to survive; she did not have enough space in her heart to question whether she was happy or not. It would have been wasted energy to ask such a question; we were married and had children to support. My fourth baby was born later when my family lived in a house on the San Luis Obispo Buddhist temple property. Her birth cost $1,500.00. Hers was the first birth I was able to cover without borrowing. I kept a receipt for her in a *senbei* 煎餅 (rice cracker) can.

Unlike my father, I kissed my babies, especially my daughter. My father and I were of different generations, and we had our children in different countries. Also, unlike my father, I helped my wife because there was no one else to help and no money to pay for medical help. After our first baby was born, I thought more about my mother and how difficult it must have been to have so many children. I realized that it is a real hardship for a woman to have a baby. Women must have pride to be able to have a baby: I couldn't do it.

At the Eto farm, there was a creek for my children to play in during the winter when the rain came. It even had a little bit of water in the summer. Throughout the year and even when the water was low, the creek had rainbow trout. During the rainy season when the creek was full of water, hundreds of three-foot long salmon came from the ocean. They escaped very quickly during the day, but at night we used a flashlight and lettuce box to trap the salmon. They splashed fiercely. Since they lay eggs during the day, if we caught them at night, they still had eggs. We had a very small refrigerator, so one was all we could store. Mr. Sakamoto knew how to prepare fish, so he did the cleaning, and we had sashimi, but the flesh was not so tasty because most of the nutrition had gone to the eggs. We cooked the fish with chicken eggs, sugar, and soy sauce and poured it over hot rice. The salmon hunting season lasted for more than two weeks. Mr. Eto waited until the salmon became weaker and used a pitchfork to spear the fish. He would pack his large freezer and give fish to visitors, like the Buddhist priest, but he didn't share with me and the other workers.

During lettuce season, I cut lettuce during the day, but at night after a quick supper break, I drove a tractor. Mr. Eto showed me how to operate the Caterpillar tractor, and I tilled the soil with the tractor. I used the Caterpillar for the remainder of my time on the Eto farm, and I would till until one or two in the morning. When I turned the switch off, in the silence I could hear my ears ringing, and they rang for at least an hour. If I scratched my check, my fingernails would be loaded with dirt, and even though I was wearing a hat, the dirt got under it. I was covered with dirt, so I took my clothes off before entering our house and shook them. I used a hose outside to rinse off, and then I would take a shower. I was afraid that breathing the fine dirt would shorten my life, so Mr. Eto gave me a mask to wear. I worked seven days a week, and the most sleep I could get at this time was five hours a night. The fact that I was in my thirties made it possible to continue on such little sleep. I

Mr. Sakamoto and I vacationing with our children at Yosemite, 1968.

wasn't sleepy in the daytime because I was driven by the family responsibility, and I would go, go, go. I couldn't complain about the soreness of muscles because it was a luxury to complain. But even with that constant work, I only made $450 a month. If Mr. Eto had hired a tractor specialist, he would have had to pay $3.00 an hour. Mr. Eto thought that was too much when he could pay me $1.25 an hour. We Japanese got a $50.00 bonus at Christmas. I came to understand Mr. Eto was stingy.

TAXES

I had zero savings; all my money was spent on living or had been applied toward my father's debt, and I still owed just under half of it. I had even borrowed for our airplane transportation, and though I had left home with only $110, my conscience was clear. However, I had not paid income taxes for two years when I was at Eto's farm.

An IRS man came and said that even if my income were low, I had to pay income taxes. So, since I hadn't paid any in two years, he was going to take some of my possessions to pay for the income tax. He said, "Is this sofa yours?" "What about the bed: is it yours?" "And the refrigerator?" I told him that it all belonged to Mr. Eto, and that only the children were mine. I showed him my bank account: there was only $5.00 left because the money was used up immediately. We had no car, and I had to borrow Mr. Eto's muddy pick-up for shopping. After the IRS agent looked around our house but could find nothing of value, he said it was illegal for him to take anything that would inconvenience me in daily life. He told me that if I were to pay him even one or two dollars, he could write that I had made partial payment. I paid $2.00 and was off the hook for moment. He told me that if I didn't pay income tax, I could be arrested. So, I learned that to avoid trouble, I had to pay something. As a gardener in Japan, I avoided paying taxes by saying I was not paid, that I was an apprentice. In Japan, all payments were done in cash. Even now Japan is a cash-oriented society. Once again, I was reminded that I was no longer living in Japan.

Disasters

One day I was tilling the soil and plowing about three feet deep. Mr. Eto had told me not to till with the tractor beyond a certain point because there was a twelve-inch water main. I had been tilling for a few hours, when suddenly, water gushed: I had accidently gone beyond the line and had ripped a hole in the pipe. I moved the tractor to keep it from getting wet, and with great fear, I told Mr. Eto. He was *extremely* angry. The reservoir that fed this pipe was in a high place, and a large wheel had to be turned to stop the water. We went to the top of the hill by car, and Mr. Eto told me to turn the wheel. He was swinging his fists and cursing saying, "God damn it, I told you!" Mr. Eto had showed a grouchy face before, but this was the first time he had gotten that angry. For one month after the pipe accident, we could not plant in that location because the ground was too wet. He did not charge me because he knew I had no money, but every time he went to the location where the pipe had been ruptured, he was reminded that he couldn't work that field. He wouldn't look at my face. I realized that Mr. Eto had a small heart: he hounded me for a month over the broken water pipe.

I was loading empty boxes one night, and it was raining. I fell on my crotch onto a trailer hitch and cut the left-hand side of my testicles very badly. My feet couldn't touch the ground, and I lost consciousness and fell to the ground. I probably passed out from pain. The guard found me, woke me up, and drove me back to camp with blood all over the place. I was simply numb. I felt something wet in my groin, and I realized that it was blood. Because I couldn't speak English, I couldn't express to the guard what I needed. The guard called Mr. Eto, and Mr. Eto immediately drove me to the hospital.

My sex organs were all torn up. The doctor operated and used tiny pipes to connect the torn parts and said I might not be able to make more babies. I was thirty-five years old and had not completed my dream of having a daughter. And I was very worried about losing my sexual ability. I asked my wife to ask the doctor about this, but she didn't want to ask. Probably the doctor said something related to this, but I couldn't understand. They gave me painkillers, and I had to carry a bag to collect urine for one month. For that entire month I couldn't control my urine. When there was no longer blood in the urine, the situation was better, and I was later able to make my daughter and last child, Jo Anne.

Disasters fell on just about everyone, even the foreman. Mr. Sakamoto had the title of foreman and was paid more. Part of his job was to record the hours people worked. If only Mexicans were working, Mr. Sakamoto only oversaw, but if Japanese were working, too, he worked. One day, Mr. Sakamoto was harvesting cauliflower. He sliced his finger with a machete so that part of the finger fell to the ground. I picked up the piece of finger and placed it on the stub and told Sakamoto to hold the two pieces together. He had lost a great deal of blood and had become pale. Another worker, Hashiguchi, and I made a tourniquet out of suspenders we were wearing to hold up our rain pants and asked Mr. Sakamoto to hold his arm higher than his heart, but blood continued to run down. Mr. Sakamoto couldn't afford medical treatment, but his finger healed after one month.

With each of my experiences with Mr. Eto, I came to understand him better. Mr. Eto was a Rotarian, and as a Rotarian he was very generous in the Rotarian sense and toward the Buddhist Church community, but he was not generous to the people who were working for him. Regardless, I owe him quite a bit because he made it possible for me to survive. After all, Mr. Eto made it possible for me to live in the United States and support my family. That is the way I started. I had no English skills and no money, but I worked very hard, and Mr. Eto gave me a job. If a job were given to me, I was thankful, and it didn't matter how many hours a day I had to work. I am aware that Mr. Eto had one face for important people and another for workers. That is one way of thinking, but Mr. Eto helped my family. But it is also true that I was not able to witness my son's birth nor see my son immediately after birth because I was working so many hours. Every year in January, I take flowers to Mr. and Mrs. Eto's tomb. And according to Japanese tradition, I told all my children that the Eto's have been helpful, so when you come home, bring gifts for the family even though the generation has changed. I wanted to show my appreciation while they lived, but they died before I could do something for them.

Tempted: The Doctor

One day when I was still working at the Eto farm, there was such a heavy rain that it was impossible to work, so my entire family went to the bowling alley to watch people bowl. We couldn't afford to bowl, but we had a good time watching. There was a man who was also watching: he was smoking and had long hair and a beard. He was wearing an army shirt, and I thought he was a hippie. He came over to us, and he patted me while Faith interpreted his question: "Are you Japanese?" I didn't like it that he touched me. He wanted to know where I worked. After talking a little while, he invited my entire family to go to his house.

His house, near Buchon Street in San Luis Obispo, had a stone wall surrounding it. We went through the back door, and there was a room with shelves packed with books. At this point, I still didn't know the man's occupation. He introduced us to his wife: I recall her very black hair, and that she was extremely quiet. She asked us if we wanted coffee, soda, or alcohol. We drank sodas, and there was lots of talk. He invited us to come back another time to visit. I told him that we didn't have a telephone at the Eto farm, but he said that he knew Mr. Eto, and he would call the Eto's house when he wanted us to visit. And indeed, one day Mr. Eto told me that there was a phone call. Mr. Eto told me the man was a doctor, Dr. K., and the message was to go to his house. We borrowed Mr. Eto's truck, and once we got to the doctor's house, there were many pairs of shoes and shirts of various sizes for my family to choose from. I said that this was too much, and I was puzzled why the doctor was so nice to us. I later found out that his hobby was to visit sales and bankruptcies. If he had gotten the clothes as a result of a store's bankruptcy, they were brand new. For three years, he helped my family in this manner, and since he didn't know our sizes, he bought lots of different sizes, and we always found something that fit.

After we got to know each other, he told me he owned property and needed help with it. He wanted me to work with him. I was puzzled why he wanted to work with me as he had a son. In fact, he had three children, one boy and two girls. The daughter married a farmer who owned property, and she raised cattle. The doctor's children were older than I and were not living at home. I asked what the son was doing, and he said he was a house painter. In time, I came to realize that the doctor's son would not have been a good partner. I felt that was the reason the doctor had asked me to work with him rather than work with his own son.

I told the doctor that I was going to become an independent gardener and no longer work for Mr. Eto. He wanted me as a partner because he needed help with his six hundred and thirty acres in Atascadero, CA, and he wanted me to help make full use of it. Because I had a background working on the Eto farm, he thought I would know how to make use of the land for a nursery, agriculture, or whatever I decided. If I signed a contract on the spot, the doctor said he would give me a gift of thirty acres. Three years passed from when the doctor had first asked me to work as a partner, and I had not given a reply. He wanted to know what was making me hesitate: didn't I trust him? Finally, I asked Faith to translate and to tell him that I hesitated because he drank too much alcohol. I told him that I had a family, and that I could not take risks because the entire family members depended upon me. I couldn't fail: I had to be certain of a steady and safe income. That statement made the doctor more eager to work with me as he saw me as a reliable person. I told him I would look at his land; I was curious, and I was tempted.

When I saw the property, my first concern was the availability of water. The doctor had two ponds that he had dammed. One pond was located at a high elevation and one at a lower. I told him that agriculture can start bringing in cash within ninety days, but a nursery would take longer to establish. I told him that I know how to grow vegetables and fruits, but I don't know how to sell. The doctor said he would oversee selling. In Atascadero, the location of his property, the summer temperature is so hot. I explained that fruit is better suited for summer, but vegetables grow better in the winter. The hot sun can burn vegetables. The doctor was impressed with my knowledge.

So, the doctor said that the land, water, bulldozers, and Caterpillars were all available, and he would pay me a salary. But I repeated my hesitation based on his alcohol habit. He repeated that we could not fail. Whenever I arrived at the doctor's house midmorning, he was already drinking. When I rode with him in his jeep, I could smell alcohol. But I knew that I would make more money working with the doctor than gardening work.

The doctor continued encouraging me to join him and asked whether the alcohol habit was my only hesitation. After I told him it was, he said to give him one year, and he would try to quit. After a year had passed, he had not quit, and he told me so, but he continued to ask me to join him for seven or eight more years.

He could not stop drinking, and his drinking led to the death of a patient. He gave a thirty-seven-year-old woman something that resulted in her death. The doctor was an alcoholic, and after the patient's death, one of his nurses reported him. His patient's death became a court case, and the nurse testified that this doctor had smelled of alcohol all the years she had worked with him. I went to court as a supporter and friend of the doctor, but I was not asked any questions. There were lots of witnesses for this case. In the end, he had to go to jail for a time. He was sued and taken to court, and he lost everything. Her death and his responsibility for it were announced in the local paper, *The Telegram Tribune*. I had associated with him for twenty years, and he had helped me. He often said, "What do you need?" He was not a bad man, but a man with a bad habit.

After being released from jail, he developed stomach cancer and became as skinny as a skeleton with his eyes sunken and bones sticking out of his face. He told me that I was the only one who came to see him, and that even his children had stopped coming. I visited him at his home, but he died in the hospital. He was probably not even sixty years old. The doctor had lost everything including his life.

Becoming Independent

Mr. Sakamoto quit working for Mr. Eto to become an independent gardener, and the week after he quit, I told Mr. Eto that I was quitting for the same reason. I went to Mr. Eto's house in the evening after work and told him I was ready to begin my own gardening business. When I told him I was quitting, he looked shocked and asked if I had been talking with Mr. Sakamoto. I had the impression that Mr. Eto thought that Mr. Sakamoto and I were trying to give him a hard time.

He became defensive, and his face tuned pale. The first Mrs. Eto, my boss' mother, came to see me three days in a row to determine why I was quitting: had her son forgotten to pay a Christmas bonus? She was concerned because it seemed suspicious that Mr. Sakamoto and I were quitting at such a similar time. Mr. Eto was very obedient to his mother and father, so if his mother had told him to take action to try to stop us from leaving, he would have. Mr. Eto did not follow the Japanese way of raising salaries, so that encouraged me to become independent; he tried to squeeze as much as possible out of everyone. So, I, who had a family to support, was eager to become independent.

After Mr. Sakamoto became independent, he had three acres to harvest, a very small amount. He asked Mr. Eto to borrow a tractor for his first harvest, and Mr. Eto refused. He said, "You quit, and I have no desire to help you." If Mr. Eto had been Japanese raised, he would have helped. Mr. Eto had many tractors and loaning one would not have mattered. In addition to that, Mr. Sakamoto was a far relative of Mr. Eto, and because of that relationship, he had a certain degree of expectation. Mr. Sakamoto was convinced of Mr. Eto's personality after that. After Mr. Sakamoto left Mr. Eto's farm, when Mr. Eto would have a party or get together, Mr. Sakamoto refused to attend. But when the first-generation Mrs. Eto was in the hospital, he went to see her. I left one week after I told Mr. Eto that I was quitting. The Japanese way would have been to have a party, a gift, and *senbetsu* せんべつ (parting gift). There was none of this.

Seven

Independence

The Buddhist Temple House

My growing family and I lived on the Eto farm from 1965 into 1970. In 1970, I started working as an independent gardener, but I needed a C27 license to work as a gardener. A three-month course held once a week on Saturdays was offered in Los Angeles. So, I began travelling to Los Angeles to study and prepare for the license exam. There was a man from Kagoshima who was teaching lessons in Japanese in his garage to five or six men who were preparing for a C27 license. I told the teacher that I needed to make money to feed my family, and that I was tired from working and then driving eight hours round trip to LA. He told me to send my wife, and she could teach me at home. So, I was able to stay home working while Faith attended classes in LA. She took our four children to her mother's home in LA, and her mother babysat the children while Faith went to landscaping school.

Because I couldn't read, write, or understand English, before Faith started attending landscaping classes, she and I had gone to

Sacramento to see what could be done about taking the test which was given in English. We found that wives were allowed to translate in a private room. When you hired your wife as a translator, she would automatically be accepted. My wife is skilled at test taking, so she attended the classes and told me that she didn't need to teach me what she had learned because she would remember everything for the test. When it was time for the test, she was my translator, and she told me what answers to write. Faith answered about seventy percent of the questions. The questions that I couldn't answer, Faith could. I passed the first time because Faith remembered everything. She got a good grade.

Three of our children were born during our time at Eto's farm, and within six years, all four of our children had been born. My first and second sons are only eleven months apart. The boys were born in this order: Jeff, Danny, and Mike. They fought much more than I did with my brothers, in part because the oldest son had pride in being the oldest, so he felt he couldn't lose a fight. My wife would often interrupt their fights. I said just watch and don't interfere, but my wife was quicker to stop the fights. Jo Anne is the youngest, but all her older brothers follow what she says, and they always agree with her.

The children's personalities are quite different from each other even though they were raised in the same home. Jeffery studied all the time whereas Danny didn't study as much, but he was efficient: he took after my wife's brain. Michael is quiet like Faith, but he took after my brain. Jo Anne talks a great deal and so does Jeffery: some people say they take after me. Danny is more like me in terms of taste: he married a Japanese woman.

The Buddhist Temple congregation owned an old house beside the temple. I was offered the house rent free in exchange for tending the Buddhist temple yard. So, my family and I moved into what was a former priest's house: a junk house where there were many rats and mice racing in the ceiling. Rat droppings were all over the place, and the baby, Jo Anne, tried to grab the rats' defecations. Once in a while small mice would make a race through the house, and I could catch them by using a grocery bag and scaring them: they ran right into the bag. My wife was very frightened of the big ones, the rats, which were about one foot long with their tails.

The temple house, a four-bedroom house with a kitchen, living room, and one bathroom, was in very bad condition. Only the living room set was already there, so I needed to buy a bed and dining table. I bought a used king-sized bed and a sofa at a place on Highland Avenue in San Luis Obispo. All my children slept on the king-sized bed with Faith sleeping at the side, and I slept on the sofa.

In the morning, our single toilet was busy, and I recalled my father's motto: "Eat Fast, Shit Fast, Move Fast." Most of my life I have needed to live by my father's motto.

On Sunday, I spent half the day working for the temple, and while we could live there rent-free, I had to pay the electricity and all other utilities. Because the Buddhist Church had plans to destroy the house we were living in so that a new house could be built for the priest, there were many maintenance problems unattended to, including peeling paint.

When we lived in the temple house, I bought a business license from the city. From 1970 through 1975, I had a license from the city that prohibited making more than $100 per house for gardening and landscaping. In 1970 it was rare that you could charge more than $100 anyway. If you were to make more than $100 from one house, you needed a D 27 landscape and contractor license. Then you could legally take care of the garden and work on designs. After 1975, I got a D 27 license. When working in the garden of a business, you must show you have insurance because the machines you use could potentially break a window or do other damage. When determining how much to charge, health and damage insurances must be factored in.

My wife's mother came to live with us, but she brought her own bed. When my wife's grandparents died, her mother inherited a large amount of money and her parents' house in Kyushu, which she sold to Susumu. The yen was weak at that time, so when she converted the money from the house sale to dollars, it wasn't much. She moved to Los Angeles to live in a one-bedroom apartment, but she didn't have enough money to live on. Her ex-husband gave her half of his social security, but that still wasn't enough. So, she got a boyfriend, and they lived together off his social security, but eventually her money was all gone: she had spent it all, and she had no work experience.

My wife's mother was skinny and gentle but strong. While I didn't like her type of person, I got along with her. Because my wife was

Jeffrey, Faith, Jo Anne, Danny, and Mike at the temple house.

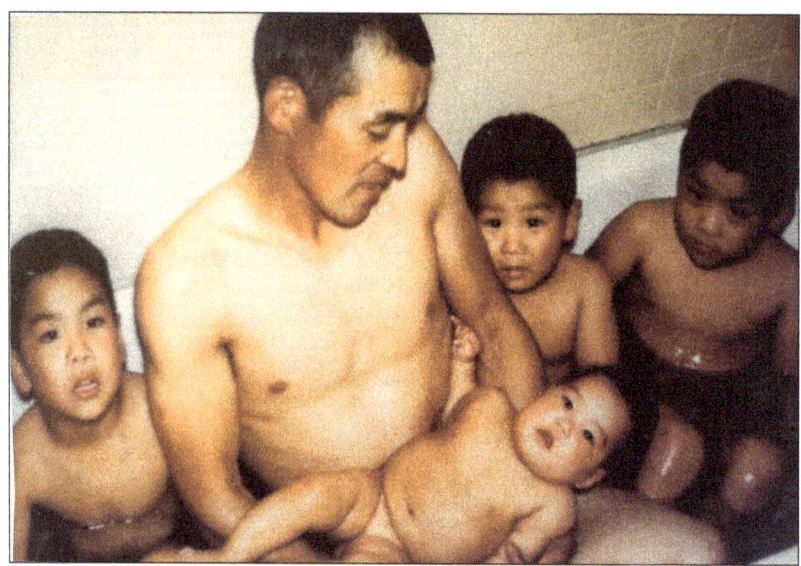

Jeff, Jo Anne, Mike, and Danny.

picking strawberries at the Okui farm, my mother-in-law helped out by babysitting; she even prepared onigiri bento おにぎり弁当 (rice ball lunch) for me to take while working. She was an honest person and optimistic, and we did not argue. She was still young, in her fifties, and capable of working, but she chose not to. It was a difficult time for all of us, but she looked comfortable, and we had plenty to eat. My children remember their grandmother as severe and firm. But she was really a wimp: I often heard laughter between her and the children. She and my wife both experienced living with money and without. When my wife lost her mother at age ninety, she didn't cry, but she did when her grandparents died.

I was concentrating on accumulating a down payment for a house. I was able to make five or six dollars an hour, so to make as much money as I could, I worked on Saturdays and Sundays as well as every weekday. Every day I worked until it became so dark I could not see any longer. My family would eat before I got home. The good pay I was earning encouraged me, and there was no comparison to my level of happiness from the Eto farm time. My work was much easier. I no longer needed to lean over in my work, and my back stopped hurting. People thought that I was working too hard, but they didn't know how hard my work had been on the Eto farm. Even with four children, I still had money left over. I kept repeating that we had to save and save and save until we could buy a house.

I collected checks from my gardening clients, and my wife kept the books. I told my wife that this is the best time to save money, and that life would start after we bought a house. She managed the money and made the decisions. I didn't even look at the checks, and I only spent money for sodas and gasoline for the car. (We had a ten-year old station wagon that cost $2000, and gas was $.29 per gallon.)

Our children enjoyed digging holes, and daily they were covered with dirt. They would dig, add water, and make pyramids out of the sandy soil; then they would firm it up and make holes with sticks. There was plenty of space for bicycle riding, so I bought Jeffery a used bicycle, and he learned to ride within two days. One day, Jeffery was going downhill, and he tumbled bloodying his face and arm. I hid so that I could watch Jeffery's reaction and see how he would handle his fall. Jeffery looked around for help, and when he found none, he didn't cry. He was in pain, and the bicycle handle was bent. I went down after a few minutes allowing time for the pain to decrease. I straightened the handle and pretended not to know that Jeffery had been hurt. Then Jeffery explained that he had fallen, and I complimented him for not crying. This is the way I handled the situation. My father, on the other hand, would have said to me in a similar situation, "You are a boy, so of course you should not cry."

We couldn't afford a television, but we had wildlife entertainment at the temple house. A family of five or six deer would come to eat apricots, wild grapes, and peaches. We enjoyed watching the deer, but the raccoons were trouble: they would take the lids off the garbage cans and make a huge mess, and the only way we could stop them was to use strong rubber to tie the lids shut. Occasionally skunks would come, and we often saw bobcats. The bobcats were larger than a domestic cat and were dark blond: they were shy and avoided us. Many non-poisonous snakes about four feet long were around our house hunting for mice.

In the rainy season, rainbow trout, about three feet long, would arrive in a creek that led to the ocean. They came to lay eggs and to fertilize them, and the creek became white with sperm. It was a shallow creek, and we would use a pitchfork to attempt to skewer the fish. I threw the pitchfork in the morning from a high location, but often the fish escaped in a pool of blood. If I got too close, they would escape. At the Eto farm, we had used a flashlight for catching salmon. But that was only during the end of the rainy season. When the water receded, the fish were more visible. The temple fish were larger than those at the Eto farm, and I only caught them once at the temple.

Temple House to Los Osos House

In 1975, after four years living at the temple house, my wife and I had accumulated $10,000 for a solid down payment on a house. I wanted a house with its own water, and my wife found one in Los Osos, CA, with a two hundred foot deep well and pump. We all went to see the house, and when the children saw it, they became extremely frisky. I had great joy seeing them playing on the stairs and lying on the floor spreading their arms. The house was on an acre: everything about it was perfect. A couple owned the house, and they were asking $75,000. They hadn't been able to sell it, and they were divorcing, so it was a good time to make an offer. The offer we made was accepted, and my wife and I bought the house. Our house was the first house to be built in that area. My initial plan was to start a nursery, so a little while later, we bought an additional acre for the nursery. There is one house between my house and the second acre. The house we bought was on an acre and cost $45,000, and the second acre cost $25,000. The second acre is now unused and covered with weeds, and I must pay taxes annually for that acre. The county took a quarter of an acre of my property to make a road, but they laid pavement.

When we bought the property, my income was about $810 a month. The mortgage was $310 a month on a thirty-year loan. I was determined I would not be sick, and that I would work seven days a week.

I was thirty-eight years old when we moved into our house. We moved from the temple house little by little every Sunday, and we used the temple truck to transfer our belongings to Los Osos. We had two trucks at that time at our disposal, so moving was easy. Plus, we didn't have many belongings and no large pieces of furniture. In fact, when we first moved in, the children didn't even have beds, so they slept on the floor. Essentially, we had no furniture when we moved in. So, every month we bought a piece of furniture: the first furniture we bought was a dining room set: a table and chairs. It had a leaf in the middle to make it larger, and it cost $18.00 at a second-hand furniture store on Broad Street in San Luis Obispo. Three years after I had bought the $18.00 table, I bought a $2000 oak table that had been handmade by a father and son carpenter team. I gave the $18.00 dining set to a man who picked it up in a truck. One month, we bought a chair that had a tear in the cushion. I have repaired it twice and am still using the chair. As time passed and we were able to accumulate a little money, I bought one of the most expensive refrigerators available that had a huge freezer.

After a while, we were able to buy and put bunk beds in a big room on the first floor of our house for the boys. All the children studied in the same room, but Jo Anne had her own bedroom. I built a chest of drawers for each of the children. The tops were triangular shaped, and I put a long board over the tops to make a study table. The drawers I made stuck, however, and the children complained and kicked at the drawers until I showed them how to yank them open. The chests are still stuffed with their junk. Number one and number two sons tell me to throw the chests away, but I will find a use for them some day. Jeffery throws things away, and then he looks for something and it is gone.

We had been able to save the down payment for the house by skipping trips to Disneyland and other sorts of entertainment. But my wife wanted us to take the children to Disneyland because the children had been asking to go, and she felt sorry for them. About two years after we bought the house, we did take them, but I had resisted, not wanting to take time off and lose income. The weekend income was important, but under pressure, I finally agreed to go.

I was shocked to see how much the children enjoyed Disneyland! I hadn't realized how happy they would become, so after all, I was glad that I had taken the day off. I had focused on the lost income, but the children showed me how to have a good time, and I learned how important it is for children to enjoy themselves. When I saw the children happy, I realized that I had been focused too much on money. When children are young, in the early grades, having fun is crucial for them. I was proud to drive them to Disneyland in a station

My mother, seated in the middle, visited us in our Los Osos house. Dairoku is to my mother's right, I to her left, and all my children are around us. She stayed one month and visited only one time.

wagon that had a new engine.

During the process of finding our house, my wife became interested in real estate. After we moved to Los Osos, she took eighteen units at Cal Poly State University, San Luis Obispo, to prepare for the real estate exam. She went to Los Angeles, took the test, and passed. After earning her license, she had to work for four years under a certified broker to become a broker. My wife worked for a woman of Japanese descent in Los Osos and after four years, she got her broker's license. Once you become a broker, you get a larger percentage of the sale price. At that time, many houses were being sold, and she did well.

With both of us working hard, the mortgage was paid off in 1995, in just twenty years.

Judo on the Central Coast

While I was still at the Eto farm in 1968, the San Luis Obispo newspaper, *The Telegram Tribune*, announced that a judo club had started. Three men, Mr. Nakamura, Dr. Kusumoto, and Mr. Brooks, were teaching judo on Higuera Street in San Luis Obispo at the former Department of Motor Vehicles building. Even if I had had the time off work, I needed a car to travel to the DMV location. I didn't have a car, so I couldn't go. Mr. Nakamura, who was from Mejei University, was the oldest, and he was a seventh-degree black belt. He planned to make a living out of teaching judo, and he did later move to Ohio where he taught judo. Dr. Kusumoto, a third-degree black belt, was the second person teaching, and he had brought a man named Mr. Brooks, a fifth-degree black belt, into the club as the third and youngest teacher. Mr. Brooks owned a pancake house in Cambria, but before that business, he had been in Japan in the United States military for six years and had gotten black belt ranks. I believe that when the United States military went to Japan, the Japanese were interested in spreading judo to the world, and they may have given black belt degrees more easily.

So, while I couldn't attend judo at the DMV location, Mr. Eto, who was a member of the PTA in the late 1960s, arranged judo demonstrations for me at Morro Bay High School. After seeing the demonstrations, some of the students really wanted to learn judo, so Mr. Eto provided a wrestling mat, and I taught for about six months. The judo students were all boys, ten of them, all of whom had wrestling backgrounds. Also, during this time, I volunteered to give demonstrations at places like the San Luis Obispo Woman's Club; Cal Poly University, San Luis Obispo; and Morro Bay High School, Morro Bay. I took Oshibuchi from Nagasaki, a man who also worked for Mr. Eto, to use during the demonstrations. I put on demonstrations three times at Cal Poly between 1962 and 1968.

It was lucky for me that rent at the old DMV increased to $500 a month and was too expensive for the club, because the dojo was moved from the former DMV to the Buddhist Temple's old school building on the Buddhist church property. The dojo had to pay rent, but it was much less than the DMV location. By the time my family and I moved to the Buddhist Temple's house, they had already been using the Buddhist Temple's old school building as a dojo for some time. Like our house, the school was in serious disrepair. As soon as I left Mr. Eto's farm in the summer of 1970 and moved to the Temple Church house, I started teaching judo at the Buddhist church dojo.

And as with our house, the Buddhist Church members were planning to demolish the school, so the dojo would have to be moved again. Dr. Kusumoto was on the San Luis School Board, and at a meeting, he mentioned that his judo club needed a building. He was told that an unused army building was available, and if the club paid the moving cost, they could have it. Even though it didn't have to be moved very far, it cost $3,500 to move the building. Mr. Truhitte, the father of two of my students from Morro Bay High School, paid for the building to be moved. I think that he appreciated the fact that I taught his sons and the others with no pay. The club got the building and location, Rancho El Chorro, San Luis Obispo, rent-free.

The first thing I noticed when I joined the Coastal Judo Club was that the judo was not high-quality judo. Dr. Kusumoto was in charge; I was a *ni-dan* 二段 (second degree black belt) when I started, but my judo education was superior. I got my black belt in 1952 in Japan, and I asked my family to send evidence of this. My family sent my certificate of *shodan* 初段 (first degree black belt) to me, and I showed Dr. Kusumoto. He was not pleased to see it because he got his black belt eighteen years after I did; therefore, I had seniority.

The Coastal Judo Club, my current club (at the time of the interview), has been in three locations. First it was at the former DMV building, then the Buddhist Temple School, and finally at the current location, Rancho El Chorro. For many years, the students at the Rancho El Chorro location were made up of little children, high school students, Cal Poly students, and adults. The dojo would often be packed with up to twenty people.

There is not always a children's class at the dojo, but the children's class is part of my agreement with the county for me to use the building rent-free. In the past, children came through word of mouth: parents communicated with each other. There is a separate class for children. I considered having the children join the adult class, but I think children should not practice more than one hour, and the adult class runs two hours.

I charge $20.00 per month to attend the Coastal Judo Club, and the price has never increased all these years. This fee covers dojo dues and utilities; I get none of it. In Japan, my judo sensei didn't charge his students; I did not know the value of my judo teacher until I had done the same thing: I have given lessons free since I started teaching. It is not an easy task, but now I am even more grateful to my judo teacher because I have done something similar to my sensei, and I understand his heart. I can say from the bottom of my heart "thank you" to my judo teacher.

Because I was trained in Kumamoto prefecture, the mecca of

Children's class at Rancho El Chorro dojo, 1980.

Children's class. Barry Bonds' uncle is the black belt standing in the last row on the far left, 1981.

judo, my shodan degree is of a superior quality to people trained elsewhere. My training had been at a very high level, and I was required to know *nage-no-kata* 投の形 (forms of throwing) to get a black belt. When Mr. Nakamura and I performed a demonstration at Alan Hancock College, after observing my nageno-kata, he became aware very quickly that I had done serious judo. Students discovered that I was a better judoist, and they turned to me for instruction. Dr. Kusumoto didn't like that. There was tension between Dr. Kusumoto and me because he felt left out. There was no spoken disagreement, but I had come later, and my rank was much more valuable than his. Dr. Kusumoto was a medical doctor and was stuck up. He quit the dojo in 1996.

Even though I had a superior training in judo, I could still get hurt.

I have gained four ranks since I came to the United States. One rank was awarded from the Southern California Judo Association. In 1970, I joined the United States Judo Federation (USJF) and became a member of the Southern CA black belt association: Nanka Yudansha Kai. But when Mr. Imamura came to the United States and started an American United States Judo Federation association (the same Imamura whom I had gone to watch practice at Tamana-city's budokan), he was required to have two hundred black belts to begin, so I transferred my membership to his association. I knew his judo quality. Mr. Imamura awarded me the other ranks. Mr. Imamura (He died September 2017.) had the right to award ranks, and he was a very righteous man; he gave no favors, not even to his own sons. He was totally devoted to judo, and his granting of rank was based on ability. He increased my rank based on his observation of my performance. He would tell me the techniques I needed to master for the next rank, and I would master them. The current rule is that you must have twenty wins to get sho-dan, the first-degree black belt. Attendance rate per year at the dojo is taken into consideration, too, although it is rare to have perfect attendance. You may participate in as many tournaments as you like to get twenty wins for the first promotion: in fact, the more the better. I am not interested in increasing my rank now, so some of my own students have reached higher degrees than mine. The fee in Japan for being awarded a black belt is $50.00, but I charge $100 since students pay less annually. Each subsequent degree costs $20.00.

Before 2002, dojos in the United States did not have to be licensed. But in 2002, the United States Judo Federation passed a law that a dojo had to be licensed in the United States. For my dojo to be licensed, I had to demonstrate knowledge of CPR, which was tested at Fresno State University, CA, through a physical demonstration and a written exam. I passed the physical part, but the written part required some help. I have a friend, a nisei, who used to be a professor. He had no idea about judo, but he was able to give me the answers for the CPR exam.

The judo spirit was much different at the time I was playing in Japan: the main goals were training and self-development. Both were gained through patience, perseverance, discipline, and respect toward elders. A judoist would be considered superior based on rank, skill, experience, and age. At the dojo, rank determines respect and is important in terms of treatment. At the time I was participating in judo in Japan, if a black belt were beaten by a lower rank judoist, he would be deeply embarrassed. Presently in the United States, each student has an individual goal: strengthen the body, win in tournaments, or lose weight. There are other goals, too. A young man named Mike was a sophomore at AGHS when he began judo. His father, a Japanese gardener in Arroyo Grande, CA, wanted Mike to learn judo because he said that since Japanese have a smaller body, they should have one physical strong point so that they feel confident in their bodies. No one can look down on a person with strength. Similarly, my father had told me that since I don't like to study, that I must be certain to have something I am proud of. The various goals of my students make it difficult to teach.

In Japan, renting a dojo is expensive which means that mainly famous and wealthy people have schools. Students who go are attracted to a big name, but if the sensei demands severe training, they leave. The instructor must pay the rent and therefore must be gentle so that he won't lose students. The dojo must be loosened

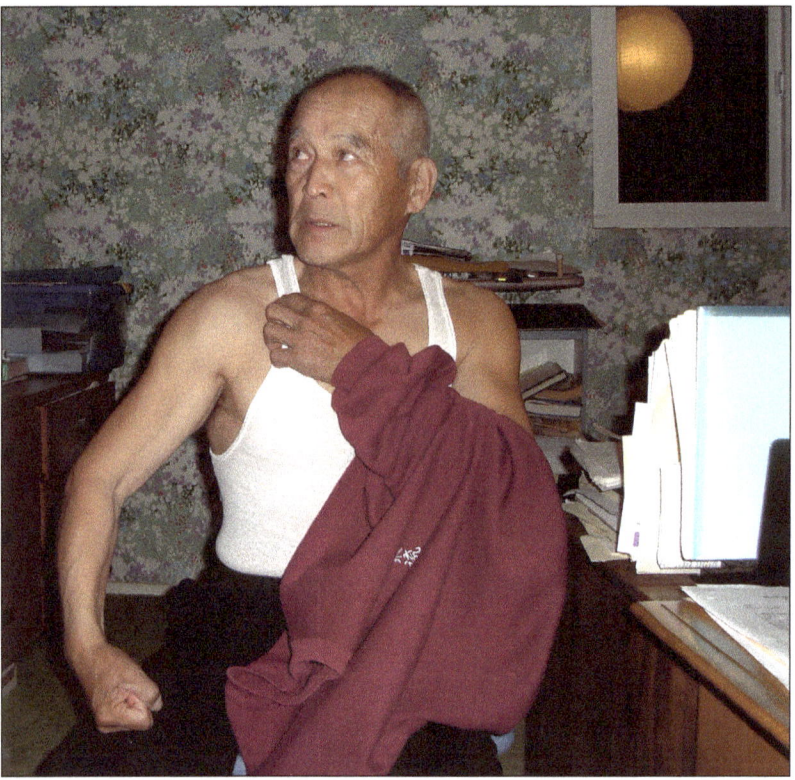

Judo Accident. I have a scar on my right shoulder that I got in the early 1970s as a result of an accident when teaching judo at the Coastal Judo Club. My nephew had come from Japan, and I was practicing with him. He threw me, and my shoulder hit the corner of a piece of wood. My shoulder was torn apart so badly that I had to have an operation. A metal bolt was inserted into my shoulder and left there along with a five-inch scar. The day after surgery, I went to the dojo and tried to teach, but I had great pain. When I am in the sun, the metal bolt in my shoulder burns my muscle with a tremendous heat, so I have to wear long sleeves as protection. I never allow direct sun to hit my shoulder. In the winter it hurts because of the cold. It doesn't set off the metal detectors at the airport, and I have no limited range of motion.

up because people are wealthy and don't feel the need for rigorous training. Japanese people don't usually quit; Americans are wealthy, so they show less interest in serious judo and are more likely to quit. Parents let children quit when judo gets hard. But on the other hand, my American students said that they would wipe the tatami mat after practice with a wrung-out rag as I had done as a student. This is not part of their culture, yet they were willing.

There were no female judo students when I studied judo in Japan. Internationally, women began judo after the 1968 Tokyo Olympics, but in *Kodokan* 講道館 (headquarter of the Judo Association of Japan), there was a women's tradition. In Tokyo and Kyoto, there were always women judoists. Keiko Fukuda, a female judoist from Tokyo, was promoted to tenth dan at age ninety-eight by the USJF. She died February 9, 2013, at the age of ninety-nine. She visited my dojo twice. She ended up in a wheelchair, but she was able to distribute medals for the National Championship from her wheelchair, and she was often invited to be a spectator. Her grandfather, Fukuda Hachinosuke, taught jujitsu to Dr. Jigoro Kano. Jigoro Kano invited Keiko Fukudo to be part of a class for women, and she became very skillful at Nage-no-Kata: both men and women went to her to learn this kata. After World War II, she moved to the United States and taught judo; she also published a book, *Born for the Mat: A Kodokan Kata Textbook for Women*, on Nage-no-Kata.

Eight

Life as a Gardener

Gardening

Before we had our house in Los Osos when I was just beginning as an independent gardener, Faith and the children were staying Los Angeles until we got a house. I had called Faith's father in Los Angeles to ask if Faith and the children could live with him for a while. He had a new wife, and he wanted to check with her. She agreed to allow them to stay two months.

In the meantime, I had to find a place to live. I had a client who was an anesthesiologist, Dr. Eugene Patrik, who said he would let me sleep in one of his not so nice rental houses free and let me park a truck outside in his yard. He put a bed in the kitchen with a curtain around it because the students who rented the house might want to use the kitchen while I slept.

I didn't have a phone, so there were no phone calls between me and Faith and the children. But Dr. Patrik offered to let me use his home phone for my business, and in an emergency, Faith could leave a message with him. One day, she called and left a message that she and the children were coming on a Greyhound bus to visit. There was no place for them to sleep, so we all slept on the floor.

When I started independent gardening in 1970, I earned $5.00 an hour. Mr. Eto had been paying me $1.25 per hour when I quit. When he found that I was planning to leave, he promised to double my salary and add a bonus if I would stay. I still would have been earning only half as much as I was working on my own.

For my landscaping job, I got up very early and worked late at night: work and money were coming with great speed. The more I worked, the more money I made. I was in my 30's: young, strong, and determined to support my family. So, I worked all day and went to the dojo in the evening. That was my life. Soon I caught on to this new way of life and often thought that I should have left the Eto farm much earlier. My income changed radically when I left Eto's, and it was a pleasure to work and accumulate money quickly. I worked seven days a week, but the fact that I had time to go to the dojo showed that I was more financially stable. Plus, my body still had lots of energy after work. Compared with the work on the Eto farm, my gardening work is so easy. I don't have to bend over as I did at the Eto's. When I drive by the Mexicans in the field, I have a melancholy feeling: that is the way I was. Each morning that I see them I don't feel sorry for them, but I know how hard it is for them. I talk to them in my heart saying, "You won't continue this forever. You can only do this when you are young." They cannot speak English, and that, too, reminds me of my young age. But they must realize that this work should not continue forever. There are many Mexican gardeners now. They have gone to the next stage: Mexicans work in the field, accumulate money, and become gardeners. The Japanese gardeners are all dying out, and Mexicans are replacing the Japanese. For Japanese, gardening lasts only one generation, because the sons of Japanese go to college.

The *issei* 一世 (first generation) Mrs. Eto had told me to save money and not buy anything new. She encouraged me to save for a down payment on a house. I did what she, as a first-generation person, told me to do. She came to the United States in 1902, and she and her husband, the first Mr. Eto, bought five hundred acres on a fifty-year loan with payments of $18.00 a month. She thought she would spend her entire life paying off this loan. After twenty years, she told me that the $18.00 was nothing. She said that in the future, the value of a home will grow. Three years after purchasing our house, I was working ten or eleven hours a day, and my income was $2000 a month. Compared with working on the Eto farm, my gardening hours were shorter, and I was earning much more money. I couldn't stop working hard: if the sun were up, I was working and would get home after dark every evening.

When I became independent as a gardener, I made so much more money than I had been making at Eto's, that I could afford a family car plus a work car. Again, I thought I should have started gardening earlier, but the reality was that earlier I didn't have the money to buy a truck. But being independent, I was able to buy a new pickup for my work: a 1970 Chevrolet that cost $2,500. It was a good truck, and I had to count on it for ten years. As with the birth of my children, I paid on the installment plan.

For the family car, I was able to buy a used station wagon from Mr. Truhitte, the owner of Truhitte Automotive, and at no cost to me, he replaced the old engine with a new one. It was his sons who had taken judo lessons with me, so along with paying for the military building to be moved for the dojo, he volunteered the engine. For ten years I had no trouble with the car because of the brand-new engine in the Ford station wagon. I have come to know a great deal about my clients, my judo students, and their families, and many of them have treated me like family and have been very kind to me.

In 1970, Dr. Patrik introduced me to a new client, Dr. K, a urologist. He told Dr K. that I didn't speak English, but that I do good work. Dr. K. remained my client until his death. He was a quiet man, but he knew and used a few Japanese words. He had worked in Japan as an army doctor for three years in Tachikawa-city near Tokyo. Both he and his wife were pilots, and they owned a Cessna. One day, his wife, who was very athletic, took me for a ride. She was a strong woman and rather harsh. Often, she would apologize for her harshness, and over time, I began to understand her personality. Her harshness stopped bothering me as my understanding of her grew. Many times, before her husband died, she told me that she was waiting for her husband's death so she could get a younger man. I worked for him for thirty-six years; in all that time, he never exercised, and in the end, he became very ill and died. He had a son and daughter, and I have known them since there were young. In fact, the family invited me to the daughter's wedding, but I couldn't go because it was December 31, New Year's Eve, and I was expected to be with my family.

I met the son, E., when he was about ten years old. When he graduated from high school, his parents gave him a one-month trip to Japan as a graduation gift. E. stayed with a doctor named Ikezono who had a son, T., of a similar age to E. E. bought a remote-control toy car in Japan and wanted to show it to me, and he wanted to tell me his Japanese experiences. Until this point, he was doing well. In fact, when he entered Cal Poly, he was still doing well.

But when E. was a sophomore at Cal Poly State University, San Luis Obispo, he told me that he planned to get married. I pointed out to him that he had no job, and he said that his wife would work. I told him to tell his parents first; when he did, there was a big fight between him and his parents. E. won, and the wedding was to be held in the back yard of a church. I was only able to attend the reception, and I waited under a tent where food had already been delivered. At 11:00 a.m., no one had showed up to the reception, and I was beginning to wonder what was going on. I thought the ceremony should have concluded. Suddenly, the bride and her bridesmaids went running by; the bride jumped in a car and slammed the door and took off. E. was chasing her and trying to stop her, but it was clearly over, and he was very upset. I still don't know if they went through the marriage ceremony or not. Dr. K's wife came out and told me that everything had been cancelled. She was extremely upset. I had never seen such an event in my entire life. As he aged, E. became an alcoholic and was good for nothing: he often landed in jail.

Faith's Position; My Position

Faith and I had no couple trouble when we lived at the Eto farm, but after we moved from the farm, she left me seven times. Jeffrey, the oldest, was in the third grade the first time she left me.

Faith wanted me to charge judo students at least $1.00 a month, and she kept hounding me about this. But I kept postponing charging a fee promising that the next year I would. In fact, I had no intention of ever charging, and I didn't consider my delay tactic with her lying. What I told her was very insignificant. Maybe the first year she believed me, but by the third and fourth years, she didn't. Charging each person one dollar was not the issue. I had confidence I was meeting my family responsibilities: I was paying our bills and making the mortgage. She just didn't understand my position. I compared my situation at that time with the situation during the war. I had food to eat and a place to live: what an amazingly fine life compared with wartime life.

My wife had been raised in a very comfortable way, and I wanted to educate her about the severity of life. I wanted to convince her that each day you can eat, you can survive. I told her that I had a big goal. I wanted to slowly improve our living situation, and then we could look back at the hardships and see how happy we were at that time. In Japan, even on her small bookkeeper salary, she could afford ballroom dance lessons because her grandparents gave her lots of money. Life with me was a huge change, but her mind and her heart are very straight, so she has grown very naturally. She doesn't sweat the little things. Having come from luxury, she must have had it much harder than I did during our most difficult years, but she still didn't understand my basic philosophy. She was already upset because at that point I never agreed to take a family camping trip, so she had accumulated anger. I had the old-fashioned Japanese man's mentality: if someone complains about minor things, ignore them. My wife said that in the two hours I spent at the dojo, if I were working in a restaurant, I could make so much money. She pointed out that I went to the dojo four nights a week. She told me that I was a nice man, but that we had a family to take care of.

It was always the same problem. The reason I refused to charge my students is because my teacher didn't charge. I wanted to experience myself the hardship that my teacher experienced by not gaining financially from my students. My motto is you don't know the meaning of hardship until you experience it. Faith had no idea what that means. She repeated that we have children and need money. I was working hard making money to support my family through gardening. If I had not been meeting our house payments or if we had had no food, I would have understood. We didn't have any savings, but I thought I was doing the right thing. Each month I met my obligations. She wanted me to change my mentality now that I was in America and no longer in Japan. She felt that if you serve, you deserve to be paid. I had my own plan how to live my life, but my wife had her own motto, and the children were her priority. There was a gap in our value systems.

Faith wanted me to change my perspective. She said that I was living life on the American stage, so I must do as they do here. She said that I was one hundred years behind. Each time she left me, always over this very issue, I told her that when her head was cool, I needed a wife and the four kids. Even though I had the urge to call when they were gone, I never did: I just waited. I was expecting my children to call, but I don't think Faith would let them. I really wanted to see them: seeing the children's faces gave me energy for the next day. Each time she returned with the children, I was afraid to ask why she came back, but I welcomed them very much when they came back. I don't know why she quit leaving me, but finally she stayed, permanently.

Nowadays, I can understand Faith's philosophy of life. The first half of our marriage, I insisted on my way, but the latter half, I have begun to understand her position. I have plenty of respect for her and am thankful for her patience. She said that if she had insisted on her way, probably things would have been very clear: get money for service, but she would not have had as many friends as she does. She is always on the phone. For example, R.G., my aiki student and friend, might call and ask her to come to New York City for a visit. When she agrees, he buys her a ticket and while in NYC, R.'s wife takes Faith around the city. This sort of relationship would not happen if R. had paid for aiki lessons. This is *ongaeshi* 恩返し (to return kindness). While I still do not charge my students, when R. invites me to his dojo to demonstrate in NYC, he charges his non-member participants, and with that money he pays for my airfare and the hotel.

My general attitude is to get to know people deeply so that I can learn their good qualities. This can only be done through a trusting relationship. I want lifelong friendships. I know Sensei Goro Kato the most profoundly. I also have other good friends: Roy, Mike, Dave, and Don. They make me happy. I don't care if I am deceived or not. If someone tricks me, then I consider it is that person's fault. So, when I feel mistreated or deceived, I know that later that person will feel the same pain. I want to understand the deepest part of people.

One morning in 1988, thirty-two of my aiki students showed up at my house uninvited. They told me to go work as usual. When I returned home from work, they had painted the inside and outside of my house. I was quite moved by this, and I asked Faith why she thought they did this. She said she didn't know; she had never experienced thirty-two people working without pay. Even though Faith was born and raised American, she has begun to appreciate the old Japanese way of life: *ongaeshi* 恩返し (to return a favor). My father's way of life was to be patient: he said to wait until spring comes, and the flowers will bloom. Be patient first.

Railroad Ties

As part of my landscaping business, I am sometimes hired to build retaining walls for my customers. One time I bought four hundred railroad ties at $9.50 each and neatly stacked them. They were eight feet by eight inches by six inches, and they could last fifty years because they were oiled. In high heat the oil oozed out, and if my children played on the ties, they got covered in oil. The deal at that time was that if you bought four hundred railroad ties, the price was reduced by twenty percent and delivery was free. I got wholesale price because I was buying for my business, but when I installed the ties, I charged retail price. I was a little worried about someone stealing the ties, so I had a home security idea: I stack the ties in a perfect shape, then if one were stolen, I could tell. I also installed a light, which turned on automatically when night fell and shone on the wood.

Four days after delivery, I noticed the shape of the stacked ties had been disturbed: I counted, and six railroad ties were missing. The next day, six more were missing. I expected that the thief would strike again. The third night, at midnight, a very foggy and cold night, I planned to catch the robber by spotting him with a flashlight and tying him up with a rope. I was thirty-five years old and in good shape; I saw this as an opportunity to practice my martial art. I called a student of mine who was a policeman, and he told me that when the man has the ties in the truck, it isn't legally stealing. I had to wait until the guy moved the truck, then he is stealing.

    I had told my wife that I was going to arrest the thief, and she laughed. I told her to watch out the window for the car, and when I caught the thief, I told her I would signal by swinging the flashlight, and she should call 911. Then she was to turn a light on after she saw my flashlight's light swinging as a sign she was calling the police.

    After about an hour, Faith yelled at me to come back in because it was cold, but I was patient believing the thief was waiting until he believed we were asleep. I hid under a bush and after almost four hours, I saw two figures coming in a Chevrolet truck. It was not a traditional pickup: the back was similar to a truck, but the front was like a passenger car. I was trembling from fear because I didn't know whether they had guns, but I talked myself into calming down. As I continued to hide under the bush, I watched as two people loaded ties. When they began moving the truck, I dashed in front of the truck and stood there writing down the license number. A guy jumped out of the truck and grabbed the paper, ripped it, and threw it to the ground. He tried to hit me, missed, and tried again. He kicked me in the groin, and I pretended it hurt badly showing how painful it was so the guy would think he had gotten the better of me. At that point I decided to break his collarbone, and after I broke it, his shoulder just bent over, and he couldn't do anything. I took my rope and looped it around the broken collarbone and swung the flashlight. Unfortunately, my wife hadn't seen the flashlight's light swinging: she had fallen asleep!! So, I began yelling for her to call the police. She woke up; she was so nervous that she couldn't dial at first, but finally she was able to dial 911.

    I had tied the guy in such a way that he was in too much pain to move. The other person turned out to be a woman, his wife, and she had remained in the car during the fight. After I got her husband tied up, she got out of the car and grabbed a stick; at first, I thought she was holding a gun. The wife tried to untie the rope, but I had tied it so tightly, that she couldn't loosen it.

    When I realized there was no gun, and she was not a man, I took a six-inch nail I had armed myself with, and I scratched the body of their car to make it identifiable. They got away while I was marking the car, and soon after, the sheriff arrived. The sheriff told me not to worry. He said to have a good sleep, and the next morning someone would come to my house with photos for me to look through and identify the thief. When the sheriff came the next day, he told me to concentrate and not to hurry to answer. I looked carefully, and finally I pointed to one and said, "This one." He said that that man was living in Templeton, about thirty miles away, and he had been to jail several times. Then the sheriff left to look for him.

When the sheriff went to the man's house, he found my railroad ties, but there were no people there. The sheriff tried to call the man, but no one answered. After four days, he visited the man's house again and asked where they had bought the ties. The man lied. He also said they were gone during the time of the theft: his said his collarbone had been broken, and he had to go to San Jose to be treated. They arrested him on the spot. After three months his collarbone healed, and he had to go to court and tell the judge what had happened. The judge asked the man many questions, and he was ultimately caught in a lie and sent to jail. I lost income because I couldn't work when I had to go to court, but the guy would not be back to steal my railroad ties. I didn't get the railroad ties back because I would have had to go get them, and I was afraid the thief's wife might have had a gun. So, I lost the ties after all. I had waited under the bush for three hours and fifty minutes, and the thief had been caught, but I still lost the ties.

Spyglass Inn and Sunset Hotel

I worked for Spyglass Inn, Pismo Beach, CA, for twenty-three years as a landscaper and gardener. There was a mini-golf course on the hotel location, and sometimes the guests walked on the garden to get lost balls. I always checked to see how much damage had been done, but regardless, I ended up being blamed. All the managers complained until they understood what was going on. One day when I was checking for damage, I found a jewelry box: a solid wooden box that held earrings and necklaces. The previous night the box had been stolen from a guest visiting from Oakland. The owner must have been in the jewelry business because it was too much for one person to own. Someone opened the box, took what he wanted, and threw away the rest. The rings and necklaces were scattered in the flowerbeds, so I collected them and took them back to the hotel and was told that I could claim forty percent of the value. I was to return the following Tuesday when I could claim my reward. The next Tuesday I worked from 8:00 a.m. until 3:00 p.m. The owner didn't show up, but the manager said he would call me when he did. A few weeks later, the manager told me that he had sent the jewelry to the owner. The police were never called, and I never did get a reward.

Spyglass had seven managers over the time I worked there. One of the managers was a young man with a business degree. He told me what and where to plant, but one time I told him that the location would be difficult to grow flowers because of the proximity to the ocean and the salty air, but that green plants would grow. But he insisted, so I planted them as he directed, and the plants died. The closest plants were just ten feet from the ocean and there was just too much salt in the air. A few weeks later the manager asked again for an impossible request. I said that if he continued to insist impossible things, I would quit. He continued; I quit. The manager called the head manager, Julie, who was aware that I had been working at Spyglass for twenty-three years. Julie asked me to continue working, but I said would not unless she fired the current manager. She thought about it but did not commit either way. In the end, she did not fire him, and I quit.

The owner of Spyglass owned another hotel in Pismo, the Sunset Hotel, and I worked there, too. I was at this location working when the manager of that hotel called me for help because an employee who was attempting to steal from the hotel was escaping. I met the thief at the entrance and threw him onto the concrete driveway and held his face down. The police were called, and they came with their siren blaring. As I was holding the guy on the cement, I recognized one of the responding policemen as one of my students, but he said not to say that we knew each other. At first, they didn't put the handcuffs on the guy, but after they questioned him, they found out that the employee had punched the manager as well as attempted to steal, and then they arrested him.

Nine

Aiki-Jujitsu

The Japanese Aiki World

TWO AIKI-JUJITSU SCHOOLS:

School: Kodokai (School of Aiki-jujitsu) Sagawa (School of Aiki-jujitsu)
Location: Hokkaido, Kitami City (split: Sapporo) Kodaira City
Director: Mr. Yusuke Inoue (former) (Shinpo) Dr. Tatsuo Kimura (Tsukuba-city)
(The American branch of Aiki-Jujitsu was formed in 1970 and became official in 1973.)

Kodo Horikawa Sensei established Kodokai in 1950 and became its president.

The same year that I started teaching judo in California, I started aiki-jujitsu. Mr. Katsumi Yonezawa, a junior high school teacher from Japan, introduced aiki-jujitsu to the Central

Coast. He started the American branch of Kodokai in 1970 and began demonstrating aiki-jujitsu. The American branch of Kodokai became official in 1973.

I had started jujitsu in Japan before I started judo, and in California, I learned aiki-jujutsu from Mr. Yonezawa. He oversaw the Kodokai school's international events. But there was a problem: he gave many promotions, and he asked for money. I was a little suspicious of both the number of promotions and how much he was charging. In 1988, a student of mine, M.T. and I went to the Kodokai headquarters in Kitami City. At the headquarters, I showed pictures of Mr. Yonezawa wearing a black *gi* 衣 (top clothing) and black hakama which only *shihan* (s) 師範 (title for senior instructors in martial arts, seventh degree and up) are allowed to wear, and I found that, in truth, he was only a third degree. He had been lying and cheating. He had faked his rank and had been promoting people to black belt degrees which he had no right to do. The names of those people who had been promoted to black belts were not registered officially. He was a schoolteacher, and no one could imagine a teacher would cheat.

Kodokai is my group, but there has been a split among Kodokai people in Japan. There are two branches of Kodokai now (in 2015): one is in Kitami City, and the other in Sapporo. Kodo Horikawa, who established the Kodokai school of Aiki-jujutsu in 1950, died in 1980, but his wife was still living in 2015. She is his third wife: his first two wives died. Horikawa didn't charge his students, but a request went out from him when he was dying, to give, if possible, financial support to his wife. So, members have been sending money to help support Horikawa's wife. Both Mr. and Mrs. Horikawa were schoolteachers all their lives. He was a school principal. My dojo's dues, which are sent to the headquarters, are $1,200.00 a year. Dojos in Japan pay more dues per month than I do. All my dues are for Mrs. Horikawa. When she became aware of the Kodokai split that led to the two branches located in Kitami City and Sapporo, she refused to take money any longer.

Currently, Kodokai is in chaos. Kodo Horikawa's wife is angry with Yusuke Inoue who was the organizational leader, because in Japan, when a person dies, there are several memorial services, and Inoue organized and performed these without letting her know, she said, where they would be located. This oversight was probably because he considered her to be such an old lady. There is a generation gap: proper manners are very important to her. When I attended one of the memorial services, Inoue had invited Tomiharu Kato, who had had a stroke, and his wife, but not the wife of the dead man.

There are three *Menkyo-Kaiden* 免許皆伝 (officially licensed instructors) presently. The three are Tomiharu Kato, Tateo Shinpo, and Yusuke Inoue who is over eighty years old now. Kato, who retired from the army and is now a salary man, has skill, but he is the youngest and therefore not considered old enough to be a leader. Being skillful does not mean he is able to lead. Since he was not chosen to be a leader, he left the Kitami City group for the Sapporo School with Shinpo. Shinpo used to be a vice president of a construction company. He has no charm as a human being; to me, he is not a quality person. In the Japanese hierarchal society, he was probably chosen because he was ranked high socially.

Presently, there are several Shihans who visit various dojos. When they travel, dues are used to pay for their hotels and flashy demonstration locations. I don't like it: they should rent a high school gym rather than spend so much money on the more expensive showy places. The young shihans want a fancy place so that people don't think that the organization is poor.

My personal goal is to develop my aiki skills. Joining Dr. Kimura's aiki group, the late Sagawa's group, would be beneficial to me, and if I were to move from the Kitami City Kodokai group to the Sagawa group, my students would follow me. I think that the Sagawa group and the Kodokai group both have true aiki, but I continue to officially belong to the Kitami City group, and it is important to me to belong to the group: since I started in Kodokai, I have wanted to continue. The modern way would be to leave because I have gained the knowledge I need, but I believe that I should continue. If a leader wants to be independent, he should have solid confidence in his skill rather than a big name and weak skill. I would rather not be independent.

What I want in a leader is aiki skill and superior human qualities. Kodo Horikawa-sensei, the founder of the Kodokai branch, was dedicated. He also had excellent skill and had a wonderful personality.

Aiki-jujitsu in the United States

Each August in San Luis Obispo there is an Obon Festival (a Japanese Buddhist festival in which ancestors are honored), and I give an Aiki-jujitsu demonstration. It is an opportunity for the community to learn about Aiki, and it is a promotional event. At the August 4, 2005, Obon Festival, in San Luis Obispo, CA, before our demonstration that day, I was looking at bonsai. A Caucasian American, about 5′ 10″ and his wife, who was about 6′, both about 45 years old and total strangers, approached me. The man had seen me the previous year at Obon demonstrating, and he said, "You guys are fake." He thought what we were doing was like what is done in movies. The man insisted that a man can't be thrown so easily.

I think he might have been showing off for his wife; regardless, I didn't like his attitude. So, I demonstrated three different throws on him and hurt him just a little bit. At that point, he accepted the reality. Earlier, this man had approached my friend and student, D., with similar comments, and I told D. that the stranger had been taken care of. When I spotted the guy in the audience of a demonstration later that day, he was watching very seriously.

Aiki-jujitsu class at the Rancho El Chorro dojo, 1990.

I don't like the American way to state an opinion on the spot without having experience. Japanese would hesitate to make such a comment without experience to back it up. In Japan, a man would come to the dojo and watch first and try for himself. Then he would have the right to say something. This guy didn't know anything about martial arts, and yet he acted like he knew everything.

Aiki-jujitsu is declining in popularity in the United States because of people like Mr. Katsuyuki Kondo, a big shot of the third generation in the direct line of Takeda Sookaku (1859 -1943, founder of the Daito-ryu Aiki-jujutsu school of jujitsu). In 2002, Kondo went to Las Vegas to teach, and seven hundred people came to learn. He had videotapes and all sorts of related material to sell. But the following year, attendance dropped to about half the original number because the attendees were disappointed. The third year, only twenty-six people showed up. Mr. Kondo asked me to take over his position in the United States, but I refused because his goals and purposes were different from mine. For Mr. Kondo, success meant to become famous and sell videos and books: a business. Marital arts are not businesses.

Aiki-jujitsu practice.

Aiki-jujitsu practice.

My opponent can no longer move.

Ten

Becoming Old, but Still Becoming

APPROACHING SIXTY-NINE YEARS OLD, AND THE DRIVING TEST: AGAIN!

My sixty-ninth birthday was coming on August 26, 2005, and I was facing a law that requires drivers seventy years old and over to go to the DMV every five years for license renewal. But before I could reach seventy years old, on two different occasions I was hit in my car from behind. Both times my car was stopped, so these collisions were not my fault. Even so, I was told I would have to take the test ... a full year before I thought I would have to! It is not clear to me why, but the Sacramento Department of Motor Vehicles said I must. If the written test is failed three times, then the physical driving test must be taken again. I took the test the first time August 9, 2005, on Tuesday and failed: I missed nine questions out of nineteen, but I passed the signals with a hundred percent. I took it a second time on August 16 and failed again missing six questions out of nineteen. I was given an extended license until September 14. If I failed again, I would have to pay $25.00 for another three chances, but even if I passed the third time, I would have to take the driving portion again. I was completely confident that I would pass the actual driving test.

The tricky questions on the test are the ones that ask for the answer that is not correct. The woman employee at the DMV suggested I try the English version, but I said that is the zero percent score kind of test. The people at the DMV were very nice to me.

On August 22, 2005, I failed the written test for the third time. I thought I knew everything, but there were seventeen questions, and I missed nine. The questions were tricky questions; for example, "Choose the one that is illegal." I thought, "Why?" I went home and told Faith some of the tricky questions, and she agreed the questions were tricky. So, I had to go back on September 8. September 8, 2005, Thursday, I went to the DMV at 9:45 a.m., and I spent three hours and fifteen minutes taking the test. It was not too busy, and they didn't interfere with me. So, after all those hours, I took the test to the counter, and I thought I would get a good result. But I had missed six. A woman working there, she looked about seventy-five years old, told me I would have to start again and pay another $25.00. The manager, a woman about forty years old, came over. She probably recognized me, and it was the first time for the older lady to see me. The younger woman said, "Just a minute. I will give you another test." It was a new one with another seventeen questions. She said that I didn't have to pay again. She circled only three questions, but it was a completely different test. All the tests were new, but the three questions she chose for me were more common-sense questions. The phrases were a little tricky, but they made more sense. It took me three hours and ten minute to answer three questions after the initial three hours and fifteen minutes! The questions looked simple, but I tried not to be tricked. I crossed out the answers that were not true. I was sweating. I was not confident about my answers on the three questions. I thought they were easy, but I wasn't sure if I were being tricked by the way they were written.

When I took the three questions to the counter to the younger woman, she didn't smile. She said that I was being given a temporary license. I asked her if I passed, but she didn't answer. Since I had already had a picture taken for the driver's license the first time, I didn't have to have another. She said that in sixty days I would get a permanent license from Sacramento. She never did smile, but she finally told me that I passed. I was drained. I felt that I had gotten a special deal. I asked her how long this would last, and she said five years. I never was so nervous in my life. When I walked to my parking spot, I was dizzy. I drank two cups of water, and then I started to calm down.

Guests, Giri, and Gratitude

VISITORS AND *GIRI* 義理 (SOCIAL OBLIGATION)

I met Mr. S. in 1997. He is a student of K., so that is my connection and the reason I accept him and his family as my guests. Mr. S. has been to my house five times in eight years. Once he asked me to pick him up at the San Francisco airport and twice at the Los Angeles airport. Both cities are about eight hours' drive round trip. Mr. S. does not ask when he can come, rather he just tells me the date that he will come. For my generation, it is difficult to say no, or I am too busy, but the younger generation might be able to say no. When I go back to Japan, friends of my generation welcome me and pick me up at the train. It is like Southern hospitality. This type of hospitality is especially true of Kumamoto people who have very warm hearts. My old friends have treated me warmly, so I try to reverse the situation as in this case. This is why I can receive others' kindness. Mr. S. was nearly fifty years old during a 1997 visit. Usually people in S.'s situation would refuse to receive such kindness, but he didn't.

On Mr. S's most recent visit, he, his wife, and their daughter, H., visited from Japan and stayed for six days. Because I took care of them the first time, they have come to expect me to entertain them and put them up at my house. When they got up the first morning at my house, my wife had left for work, so I took them out for breakfast, and I paid. The next day I took the S. family to Yosemite, and I only got two hours sleep because it is such a long drive to Yosemite. I paid for gasoline, which was $82.00 round trip. I also had to hire one of my students to take over my work. When we got back, I was too tired to take them to Universal Studios, which they had asked to see, but promised to take them another day. I took them to the Morro Bay Museum to see the sea elephants instead, and then my wife took over at 3:00 p.m. to take care of them. She never criticizes anyone or anything, and it is very difficult for her to say no. If she must say no, she will ask me to substitute for her. She took them for sushi, to Farmers' Market, and then took them back to our home. The next day they spent in town: I left them there and they shopped; later, I picked them up. The day after that, I got up at 5:00 a.m. to take them to Universal Studios. Mr. S. couldn't help with the driving because he had violated traffic laws in Japan and had had his license taken away. For that trip, I lost $140 for two days' work, plus I had to pay my replacement. I wouldn't expect anyone else to do for me what I was doing for S. This is not *giri* 義理 (socially pressured duty) as I owe him nothing, but rather I take care of him and his family because Kimura introduced him to me and asked me to take care of him.

In all, I lost eight days of work because of my guests. I had driven the visitors around for four of those days; it took twelve hours of driving round trip to Yosemite and ten hours to Universal Studios round trip. My blood circulation is not very good because of my sugar diabetes, and my legs were swollen after the many hours of sitting and driving.

Mr. S. and his family left on a Sunday morning, and that afternoon I went to sleep at 4:00 p.m. I went to the bathroom during the night, and my ankle was feeling odd. Monday morning, I got up and the ankle was extremely painful. I did go to work, but at 2:00 a.m. Tuesday, I went to the bathroom and my ankle was throbbing. Usually if I have pain, it will go away in a few days, but this felt very different, and I was afraid. A few hours later in the very early morning, I called R., my aiki student and friend. He is a physical therapist. He asked me how I was, and I told him that I was no good. R. said to put ice on the ankle, but we had already done that for half an hour. I was concerned because I hadn't done anything that I was aware of to cause this pain. I went to the emergency room, and this was the first time in my life I had initiated a trip to the emergency room. I had awakened my wife at 4:30 a.m., and we left for Sierra Vista Hospital at 6:45 a.m. My wife stayed with me until 1:00 p.m. but had to leave for work.

I had to sit and wait for a long time. After I finally saw the doctor, he called in a specialist who numbed my ankle and extracted fluid. Before the fluid was removed, there was a great deal of throbbing, but after it was removed, the pain was gone.

The fluid was dark yellow, and the doctor said that the fluid would have to be tested. I had to wait four hours for the results. It turns out that I had an infection between the bones. A specialist arrived at 8:05 p.m. and said that I had to choose between taking medication only or surgery. I chose the operation. At 9:10 p.m., the nurse put a mask over my face and then gave me a shot. The shot put me right out, but at 2:10 a.m., I woke up to find lots of ice on my foot. I had had zero to eat. I had had only half a cup of green tea before leaving home for the hospital, and I had had no lunch. At 7:45 a.m., the nurse brought one sausage, one muffin, and one egg. She also had Lipton tea. I asked for more food and was given orange juice and five crackers. The nurse put an IV in my arm, and then I didn't feel hungry. The doctor was about forty-five years old, tall, and very gentle. I would have preferred Dr. Hayashi, but this doctor was a specialist in microsurgery. I didn't have an interpreter for the specialist. The doctor understood most of my English, but I only understood about thirty percent of the doctor's. I was finally released on Thursday morning at 10:00 a.m.

Because the guests were coming, we had been cleaning, and my diabetes medication was in a different place. I lost my routine, and I had not taken my diabetes medication for nine days. I am not angry: it is over. It was my mistake to have misplaced my medicine, and it taught me a good lesson. I am very good at not getting upset in cases like this. When I interpret something very negatively though, I get very upset. And if I go in that direction, I can feel anger. The nurse asked me if I were under stress, and I told her about a driving test I was required to take (another one) and how stressed that was making me. When I was on crutches, I had time to study for the test; I had no other stressors. But I can't control the stress about taking the driving written exam because I have failed so many times. I think life is learning.

GRATITUDE

I know that not everyone feels the way I do: Some people who have become successful who worked for Mr. Eto have no gratitude toward him. I think it is natural when people become equal financially that they tend to forget their gratitude. They forget the help they received, but people should not forget. It is really thanks to others that one can live, so I see society as a structure for helping each other.

When we were at the Eto's, we did not have money to buy birthday cakes for the children, so we bought a single cupcake, put a candle in the middle, and cut it into many pieces to share. When we cut the cupcake into pieces, the children were happy, but when my grandson turned seven, he had a $50.00 cake and there was not even a smile, and the adults complained it was too sweet. I was totally puzzled. My children were always so delighted to see the tiny slice of cupcake, and they were in a hurry to eat their piece.

I have also been puzzled by the lack of enthusiasm when my grandchildren receive gifts. I have never seen my grandson delighted. He gets something, says thank you, and puts the gift aside. In general, people today don't have keen happiness. I was very appreciative of everything when I was growing up: poverty saved me and made me strong. My wife and I made children, had obligations and responsibilities, and had to work. I made my children, so there is no choice but to support my family. Responsibility made me a strong man and gave me lots of energy. I was sure I would never get sick because I was too busy to get sick. I believe not having enough is better than having everything. I don't think that my grandchildren feel gratitude or thankfulness toward their parents because they take everything for granted. It is a matter of fact: childhood circumstances affect how people perceive society.

My Seventieth Birthday
August 26, 2006

I don't like looking older.

By my seventieth birthday, I had lost both of my parents. When my father died, November 12, 1967, I missed his funeral, because, I found later, my father's request to my mother when he thought he was dying was to not let me know of his death until one year after he was gone. He knew that my condition was difficult in the United States both financially and mentally. He was afraid that I might not be able to handle more bad news. I think his idea was the correct one. But ten months after my father's death, a friend called me saying that I must feel discouraged now that my father is dead. That is the way I found out that he had died. September 8, 2004, 3:00 a.m., Japan time, my mother died. I was not able to attend her funeral, either, but I heard later the funeral was very crowded. There is a law that cremation can't occur before twenty-four hours after death, but any time after that is permissible. I would not have had time to get back for the funeral and cremation as both occurred soon after her death. My mother was my teacher: I realize that now because the way I parent is very similar to my mother's way. My parents were both gone, and I was turning seventy years old.

I had my seventieth birthday party on August 26, 2006. The party began around 2:00 p.m. at the Buddhist Temple, the temple location where we used to live. There were many people from various areas of my life: family, grandchildren, aiki and judo students, friends, and friend's children. My son, Mike, however, was not there because his car needed to be repaired. He had been promised it was a two-day job, but it ended up being a four-day repair. There were gifts, too: a wind chime, jacket, water filter, money gifts, a gift certificate to Tsurugi's Japanese restaurant, a karaoke machine, and more. My children and Jo Anne's husband prepared the food for a noon meal. There was enough money from gifts for me to buy an Enka CD.

D.P. gave me a handprint of Mr. Kodo Horikawa, but I told D. that after I die, it goes back to him. He asked me to make twenty of my own *shikishi* 色紙 (thick paper board). Using traditional red ink that is used for the *hanko* はんこ (stamp used in place of a signature), I made twenty handprints on twenty thick boards. After they dried, I signed them and sealed them with the Kodokai seal.

At 7:00 p.m., Faith told everyone to come in and eat. Dinner was miso soup and leftovers from lunch. After dinner, only the aiki people and my family remained. Finally, at 10:40 p.m., the party was over. I was very moved by my seventieth birthday, in part because there is some kind of sadness associated with it. I was happy, but I was aware that I was seventy years old. I was thankful, however, to the people who had prepared; I was also thankful that I had reached seventy years old with few physical problems.

I didn't feel important by the large number of guests who attended, but I was more convinced that my continued judo and aiki had not been a failure, and I was glad that I had continued all these years and was content with what I had done. The reason the people came to the party is because they had gained something from judo or aiki, or that I had influenced them in some way. When I was young, I was busy making money to support my family, but when I reached my forties and fifties, I noticed that I became more human because, I think, death is getting closer and closer. Probably people who have met me in the past may more recently sense my change to more human behavior, and they might have been influenced by that change.

R. tells me that meeting me has been crucial for his life. I have changed him, he said. D.P. and R.E., two of my aiki students, expressed a similar attitude. I am grateful toward all these guys because they helped me during my financially hard times. The true value of a person will be made clear after that person's death: a person can't self-proclaim importance.

Eleven

Concluding Thoughts

As a child during wartime, I had one goal: to eat; so, I was focused on fishing and getting food. I had no freedom to dream as a child. When I was in junior high, the war was over, and my dream was to become an Olympic star in the one-hundred-meter dash. But because of my father's stroke and having to repay his debt, I had to work and could not go to high school, which I would have had to do to enter the Olympics. My dream today is to retain my current health, not to become richer. For the coming ten years, I am concerned with how to live healthfully with no operations and without needing a doctor.

When I was a teenager, I thought that my adult life might be even worse than it was at that time, and I thought about ending my life. But great joy that I didn't hope for or expect awaited me. Today, each day is filled with pleasure, and I have concluded that thanks to poverty, I could reach the level of happiness I have today.

During my first years in the United States, I was keenly aware of my poverty, but the situation I was in didn't allow me to brood on it. Thinking about my situation was replaced with hard work, and all I could do was to continue working hard. After three years, I decided I wanted to return to the United States and to this hard work. When

I came to the United States, Mr. Eto said that the United States was twenty years ahead of Japan, and indeed, each American family had two cars, but in Japan, families had no cars. In Japan, getting a new bicycle was a great event.

My children's lives are different from what my life has been, so when they were growing up, they questioned why they couldn't do what other children were doing, like taking vacations. When Jeffery was seventeen, Danny sixteen, Mike fifteen, and Jo Anne twelve, I had my wife gather the children, and I decided to explain why we couldn't afford trips and vacations. I was ready to talk, and with a dessert in front of them, they were ready to listen. I told them I was not well educated, and if they didn't want to work seven days a week as I have had to, they had better go to college. I encouraged them to go to college not for me but for themselves. I had been preparing them for this day. From eight years old, on Saturday and Sunday, I took my three sons to work with me raking leaves and carrying the gathered leaves to a garbage can. At age fifteen, I bought each of the children a bicycle so they could ride to Ralph's grocery store to carry groceries and get tips. They were ready to listen, and by age fifteen, they were able to understand what I was talking about.

For many years I was busy solely with supporting the family and not aware of much else, but recently I appreciate Faith's efforts to raise our four children. My appreciation is strong. Who I am now comes from her effort and patience. She worked hard to raise our children. Now I naturally rub my wife's back as an expression of gratitude. When we watch TV, sometimes there is a scene in a drama that reminds us of how we were, and my hand, without planning, comes up to rub her back to say thanks for how hard she worked for the family. I am convinced that I need to be aware of her needs, so I am doing whatever I can to make her happier and to please her. Whenever she wants to travel to see the grandchildren, I agree without hesitation. If she wants to go to a grandchild's soccer game, I always happily go. What she desires is now my job to satisfy. I plan to tell her in words my gratitude, but I am waiting until I have a terminal illness. If I tell her now, she will think I am deathly ill. As a joke once in a while I hint about my gratitude, but I can't be too serious about it. I use TV drama moments to say what I really want to say.

I don't have very good things to say about myself: it was my duty to raise my children properly. I can't think about my strengths or be proud of them, and I refuse to admit my weaknesses!

Life is natural. I did not ask for life, and I didn't plan for it: simply, life was given. I just followed the path I was given. One of the determining factors in my life was my responsibility to return my father's debt. I had no choice, so there is no point looking back and wondering if I could have done something differently.

It was my choice, however, to return to the United States, and it was also my choice not to inherit. Since it was my choice to return to the United States, I felt that I should repay my father's debt; otherwise, I would have felt guilty for leaving the debt for my family without having helped repay it. So, to be allowed to leave with a clear conscience, I thought that it was my duty to work to pay off my father's debt, and then it would be easier to say I won't be back. I returned eighty percent of the debt. His debt was paid off in 1968.

I am happiest now: my children are grown, and my wife and I have no disagreements. My life is without anxiety and trouble. Family is most important: if my family members are living healthfully and happily, then life is perfect.

I don't have a right to tell others how to live life, and I have no message for others about how to live life: I have lived my life the way I have because I was living under a specific set of circumstances. I had no choice.

Eto fields where I worked.

"... thanks to poverty, I could reach the level of happiness I have today."
—Hayawo Kiyama

www.ingramcontent.com/pod-product-compliance
Lightning Source LLC
Chambersburg PA
CBHW040312170426
43195CB00020B/2941